Le Roy Tales From The Old Brown Table

Quaint Stories of a Le Roy, New York Family in the Early 20th Century

William J. Brown

To My Darling Wife
Mary Ann

Cover designed by Joe Pohorance
First Edition 2020 © William J. Brown
All rights reserved.

Table of Content

Dedication	vii
Acknowledgements	viii
Abbreviations	ix
Forward	x
Introduction	1

Chapter One 1890 to 1920 Old Brown Table Tales	3
What, Bad Salt at the Lehigh Mine?	3
Fanny Was Run Over by a Train	6
Those 1916 Wedding Bells	8
Chapter Two 1920 to 1930 Old Brown Table Tales	10
Donald Woodward Airport Opening	10
1929 Year of Activity for D. W. Airport	14
Amelia Earhart Is Coming To Le Roy	19
Ford Model T Wreck	22
Golden Celebration at the Old Brown Table	24
Oh, Cow Where Art Thou?	25
Talking Movies	27
Chapter Three 1930 to 1940 Old Brown Table Tales	30
Come Play with Me	30
Frank, You Captured My Clothesline	31
Slap on the Back	32
Sunday Noon Spaghetti Dinners	33
The Head Hole	34
Chapter Four 1940 to 1950 Old Brown Table Tales	36
Al Won a Farnsworth	36
Aunt Katies	37
Baby Woodchuck	38
Black Hawk Was Here	40
Can Mom Climb A Cherry Tree?	43
Charlie McCarthy Talks	44
Chemistry Set	46

Dad Fell Off the Roof	47
Ellis Chocolate Easter Egg	49
Front Yard Antics	50
High School Renovation Hazards	53
Horrific Grind	55
Jack, Do You Believe in God?	56
James P Tountas	61
Le Roy Theater and Adorable Cheeta	63
Limburger Stink	64
Main Street Fire	65
Missing Only Two Months	67
Mom, Mom, I Struck Gold in the Sandbox!	70
My Eyes, My Eyes	72
Parking Meter Dilemma	73
Pie Plant Pete & Bashful Harmonica Joe	75
Red Ryder Run	78
Religion & White Sand	79
Richard Longhany Is Missing	82
Salmon on Ice With 1720 Wine	83
Skiing is Fun, but Skating is Worse	85
Smoking 49 Chevy	87
St Joes Call Back	89
Strike at Lapp Insulator	91
Swimming at the Ole Swimming Hole	92
The Loss of a High School Classmate	94
The Red Cross Letter	95
The Fateful Telegram	98
Undulant Fever	100
What Is That Scar Frank?	101
What, Held Back in The Seventh?	103
Where Are the Statues of the Saints?	106
Who Left the Car Door Open?	107
Who Rang the Dinner Bell?	109
Woman's Scream on A Cold Winter Night	111
You Bought a Hoover?	112
You're Going to Shoot Your Eye Out Kid!	113
Chapter Five 1950 to 1960 Old Brown Table Tales	116
A Girl Named Barbara	116

Billy, You Are All White!	117
Blow Out	120
Darlyn What is Wrong	121
Don't Drink the Water	122
Fire-Fire!	123
Grapes, Grapes, Grapes	125
Hazardous Field	126
Home Movie Nights	128
Is That Gas I Smell?	129
Leaning Tower of Pisa	131
Fire in the Hole	133
Model T Buzz	135
My Reckless Neighbors	136
Place of a Thousand Names	138
Salt Mine Oil	141
Sky Snakes	143
That Mysterious Silver Metal	144
That Old Accordion Player	145
The Woodward Legacy	147
Unusual Table Foods	151
What is That Horrible Noise? The Doodlebug	152
Who Can Forget the Laughter?	153
You Sliced Off the Fenders?	155
Chapter Six 1960 to 1970 Old Brown Table Tales	**157**
A Day of Adventure at Grandma's House	157
Christmas at Grandma Browns	160
Cookies and Milk	162
Ghostly Children at Play	163
Grandma Brown's Hot Chocolate	166
Grandma Brown's Magic Kingdom	167
Oh, Tara You Should Be Ashamed of Yourself!	168
Over the River and Through the Woods	170
Weapons of Choice	172
Epilogue	175
About the Author	177
Connect with the Author	178

Dedication

This book is dedicated to the citizens of Le Roy, New York, who, throughout the years, have devoted their God-given talents for the benefit of their families, the community and the nation. Their courage and vision led to the development of several varied industries during the late 1800s and early 1900s, offering employment for the arriving immigrants. The community leadership brought Le Roy into the 20th Century with various manufacturing, business establishments, educational institutions, an airport and related services. The factory laborer, farmer, business owner, educator, community leader, and clergy share the credit for the development of an exceptional community that spans two centuries.

Although Le Roy encountered adversity through the years, such as fires and loss of manufacturing jobs, the town has always responded with courage and a positive attitude toward the future. Le Roy is a shining light of small-town USA, where one is proud to live and raise a family in a neighborhood-friendly environment.

Acknowledgments

The author gratefully acknowledges the support of his loving wife, Mary Ann, who offered encouragement throughout the writing of this book.

The author's family and friends, which include Mary Ann Brown, Frank Brown, Richard Brown, Robert Baroncinni, Christopher Baroncini, Darlyn Costa Hawkins, Marilyn Costa Pocock, and Janice Morgan Youngman. They all provided memorable events at the Old Brown Table and many helpful comments.

My son Robert providing counsel on the construction of narrative.

Lynne Belluscio, Director of the Le Roy Historical Society and the Jell-O Gallery Museum, for providing several photos used in this book.

Abbreviations

B&O	Baltimore and Ohio Railroad
Deg-F	Degrees Fahrenheit
D. W.	Donald Woodward
LRGN	Le Roy Gazette News
LRHS	Le Roy Historical Society
WikP	Wikipedia

Forward

In the fast-paced life we live today, do you sometimes wonder what life was like fifty or a hundred years ago living in a small rural town? Maybe you talked to your senior family members or viewed movies and TV specials depicting life in the early 20th Century. The author has attempted to describe family life in those early days through a series of tales, which occurred in Le Roy, a small rural town in upstate New York. Some of the tales are humorous, joyful, and a few tragic.

The tales are witnessed by the Old Brown Table, where countless conversations occurred over eighty years and provide a historical perspective on family life in Le Roy. Yes, if the Old Brown Table could only talk and relate those precious conversations.

May you laugh or shed a tear or two and gather a deeper appreciation for life in time past.

Introduction

I had the advantage of growing up in a small town in upper New York State called Le Roy, where everyone almost knew everyone in times that today would be considered slow and simple. We lived two miles south of town on Warsaw Road (Route 19) occupying a small farm acquired by my grandparents Charles and Mary (Baroncini) Brown, in 1903 from J. L. Johnson Farms. The homestead was built from two homes purchased and moved from the abandoned Lehigh Salt Mine just one-quarter mile down the road. My parents Jack and Nellie Brown, raised their family on this small farm, becoming lifetime residents of the Le Roy community.

In the old homestead, there was a small kitchen with a large oak brown table upon which we enjoyed our meals and discussed many a current topic over the years. Have you ever gazed upon or admired an attractive piece of antique furniture and wondered what it witnessed as it served its purpose over years of use? If it could only talk and reveal events in the local community along with conversations of family and relatives experiencing personal, humorous, and tragic times. This book centers around this Old Brown Table and tells ninety tales that occurred for over 80 years of family life in the Le Roy community. Each story is unique, with some recalled by family members, some by the author, and some enriched and collaborated by the Le Roy Gazette News, which in those days was the equivalent of Facebook today. Families would use the local paper to announce their daily life activities, who visited who, illnesses, accidents, and anniversaries.

This book will entertain you with memories of small-town life in the early 20th Century and provides examples of individuals that made significant contributions to the Le Roy community. We should be forever grateful to our town benefactors for their offerings over many years such as the Woodward philanthropy. As you read this book may you enjoy and live these experiences as I have through the years.

Chapter One

1890 to 1920 Old Brown Table Tales

What, Bad Salt at the Lehigh Mine?

As a young boy I was intrigued by the remnants of a salt mine just a half mile south of the old farmhouse on Route 19. The land was in use as a pasture for the cows on the Johnson Milk farm, which helped to keep the field clear of brush and trees. You could view long concrete foundations where buildings housed the salt after it was extracted from deep below the surface and a rectangular opening surrounded by a chain link fence that housed the mine shaft. On a hill close to the B&O railroad tracks there was a submerged brick lined tank about 20 feet in diameter and eight feet deep for storing water for processing salt.

I did not realize at the time that this was the site of the Lehigh Salt Mine, where construction was started in 1884. Theodore F. Fuller in recalling his life in Le Roy during the years from 1891 to 1894, as reported in the Le Roy Gazette dated January 4, 1945, said he had very pleasing recollections of his experience in Le Roy. He came to Le Roy with the Lehigh Salt Mining Company to operate the mine two miles south of the village. He said the company was financed by Pennsylvania capitalists in conjunction with the Lehigh Valley Railroad. The general manager Edward K. Fuller of Scranton PA was a cousin of Theodore Fuller. Edward Fuller operated an anthracite coal mining business in Pittston, PA, and his company sold a large shipment of coal to well-known coal dealers in Le Roy. However, one cargo of coal did not meet the quality expected, and the Le Roy dealers refused to accept it. Edward Fuller then came to Le Roy to settle the matter and asked for the smartest lawyer in Genesee County and was directed to General C. F. Bissell. Since the production of refined salt was a significant business in Le Roy, General Bissell interested Fuller in developing a salt mine, which was very similar to the mining of coal.

The first step was the purchase of several hundred acres of farmland and several thousand acres of mineral rights for $10 per acre. A few farmers in May 1891 would not agree to the options price and took their cases to court petitioning for a higher price based on the salt below their property. Before this, a diamond drill had removed a four-inch core at 700 feet down that showed that salt was present. After passing through a layer of shale, a layer of gypsum is usually encountered, followed by flint and limestone rock. At the Lehigh Mine, salt was discovered at 700 feet, and the shaft went through 22 feet of rock salt, which was in four different layers. The first layer was seven feet, the second three feet, the third and the fourth was six feet each. The 12-foot vein was the vein that was mined although the 7-foot vein was brighter in color but mixed in with pebbles and small pieces of shale.

The sinking of the shaft was undertaken, 13 feet wide and 24 feet long. The shaft excavation was a slow and tedious process on a three eight-hour shift, seven days a week, taking about a year to complete. In August 1992, the shaft reached salt at 804 feet with four veins totaling 22 feet. One vein 12 feet thick was dark grey. Upon processing, it was determined to be of excellent quality with the color of powdered sugar. On this date, salt mining was officially commenced with the first shipment by railroad.

In April 1992, building construction began, including ten new company houses on the west side of the railroad along with a large boarding house. Company houses and a boarding house were also built across the road on Route 19. At the same time, the plant was under construction for screening, mixing, and scoring the rock salt. A rock salt breaker was constructed, which was 125 feet high and equipped with crusher screens and a large storage bin arranged, so the salt was crushed and dropped by gravity to the bins and from there to the B. R. & P. freight cars. The freight trains would transport the salt to stockyards, soap factories, chemical plants, ice cream companies, leather manufacturers, refrigerator car use, soda ash manufacturers, streetcar companies, railroad lines, etc. At the turn of the century, there was a wide industrial need for salt, and the demand was high.

A large portion of the salt was shipped in boxcars in bulk and open gondola cars to Rochester and then via the Erie Canal. Much of the salt was shipped in bags of 50, 100, 200- and 230-pounds weight. The plant was all steam heated, electricity lighted, and had its water system fed from the reservoir on the hill. The buildings of the plant included the salt breaker, concrete reservoir, machine and carpenter shop, engine steam shop containing the hoisting engines, and a large brick boiler house. The entire enterprise required an expenditure of $800,000 before actual mining of salt was underway. In 2020 dollars, this is equivalent to $22,700,000, which is a substantial expenditure for any enterprise.

The plant began full operation in October 1892 and was operated for about one year when the salt mining industry in upper New York State took a dramatic change. The Retsof Mining Company in Retsof, NY, had been in operation for several years and was able to supply the rock salt demands for the country shipping 1000 pounds of rock salt per day. In 1891 three separate salt mine shafts were sunk, which included the Lehigh Salt Mining Co., Livonia Salt Mining Co., and the Greigsville Salt Mining Co. After two years of operation, all three were shut down in 1893 and never reopened. On November 14, 1894, the deed was conveyed from Lehigh Salt Mining Co. to Retsof Mining Co., together with $800,000 in mortgage bonds. The Retsof Salt Mining Company stayed open and eventually became the International Salt Mining Company, which remains open to this day.

Now many a story was told at the Old Brown Table just a half-mile down the road. Across the street from our farmhouse was a home where Andy Meehan resided. He was brought in by the Lehigh Salt Mining company as an expert in excavating the 700-foot shaft. He told my grandparents that the salt quality was excellent. However, the salt company said the salt was discovered to be of low quality, and therefore they abandoned the mine. Now it is challenging to believe that the Lehigh Valley Railroad would invest almost $800000 if they knew the quality was poor. What they did not foresee was the overproduction of salt from five salt mines.

After the closing of the mine, two houses were purchased in 1903 by my Grandparents Charles and Mary Baroncini and moved a half-mile down the road to form one home on nine acres of farmland. The Brown Homestead is where I was raised as a child and in the kitchen resided the Old Brown Table.

LRGN: 4-27-1892; 8-8-1892; 10-19-1892; 11-8-1893; 11-14-1894; 1-4-1945.

Fanny Was Run Over by A Train

In 1903 the Charles and Mary Baroncini family moved from Buffalo to Le Roy. Charles had experience working in salt mines and the salt industry in Le Roy would provide him ample opportunity to find work. Mary was tired of living in the city and wanted to settle down on a small farm where they could raise vegetables, fruit, have chickens, pigs, and a milking cow. Mary was tired of scrubbing the floors of Pullman cars in Buffalo, and through her hard labor, they saved enough money to buy a small country home.

With friends in Le Roy and Lime Rock, they learned about the Lehigh Salt Mine shutting down, and there was an availability of company homes that would be sold. In those days, it was common for a company to build housing for its employees since transportation was limited to the horse and buggy for short-distance travel. Le Roy was known in the late 1800s for the production of salt using the process of evaporating brine, which is

Baroncini Homestead 1905

mined rock salt mixed with water. At this time, Charles and Mary bought nine acres of land on Route 19 from J. L. Johnson Farms and purchased two houses from the Lehigh Salt Mine, which were moved about a half a mile north to the new home site. The two houses were placed together to form a nice size homestead that fulfilled the dreams of Charles and Mary for many years. They had two children living with them at that time, Jacob called Jack, and Francis called Fanny. One of their first furniture buys was the Old Brown Table, a fine oak kitchen table that could be expanded with three leaves to a length of eight feet.

On Saturday, December 9, 1905, Fanny and her neighbor girlfriend, Ruth McDowell, decided to walk to town along the B. R. & P. railroad tracks that ran on the back-lot line of the Baroncini homestead on Route 19. Route 19 was likely mud and ruts in December since it was a gravel road, and it would be easier walking along the railroad tracks. On the railroad tracks, they had to cross O-At-Ka creek on a trestle just south of Red Bridge. It was a long span about 30 feet above the stream, which was shallow and more likely covered with ice. The two girls reached the midpoint of the trestle when they saw an engine and caboose coming along at a high rate of speed. They realized that they did not have time to get off the trestle, so with quick judgment, Ruth McDowell reached the end of the trestle ties where she held herself over the creek until the train passed. Fanny without thinking lay down between the rails expecting every moment that she would be caught by the engine and killed instantly. The engine and caboose passed over her without injury except her raincoat was caught and torn into pieces.

Fanny Baroncini

Fanny's mom, Mary, was at the Old Brown Table when she first received the news that Fanny was run over by a train but is okay. Mary was startled, worried, and confused. How could the train run over her, and she was not severely injured or killed? When the horse and buggy brought Fanny home, her dad and mom with relief warned her never to attempt that feat again. The Old Brown Table witnessed happy moments that evening.

LRGN: 12-19-1905.

Those 1916 Wedding Bells

Dad, Jack Brown, obtained a marriage license on February 12, 1916 and the plan was to marry his fiancé Nellie Stefani on Saturday, February 26, 1916, at St. Anthony's Church in Lime Rock, two miles east of Le Roy. However, mother nature had a different plan producing a very severe snowstorm on Thursday, February 24th. The storm began with rain, which froze as quickly as it fell, placing a coating of ice on everything. It then turned to snow with a foot on the ground by Friday afternoon, and with falling temperatures, it continued to snow until there were 17 inches on the ground. Dad phoned Nellie at the Gulf Hotel operated by her father that the wedding had to be postponed much to their disappointment. Then Saturday night, gale force winds developed and blew the snow on Sunday to huge drifts blocking almost all roads. That is when plan B went into effect with the wedding postponed until Wednesday, March 1st. However, the problem remained on how to get to church since there were few county plows in those days.

My Dad's first car was a 1916 Model T Ford, which he bought when he was 24 years old and preparing to marry my Mom. Now to purchase a car in the early 20th century was indeed bold since very few people had cars. The Henry Ford Model T four-door was ideal for the workingman even though it could only be realistically run in the warm weather. It had to be hand-cranked to start and would be very difficult to use in the upper New York state winter climate. Roads were not plowed and salted as they are today since the primary mode of transportation was by horse and buggy, which could navigate snowdrifts by traveling off the road through the farmer's field.

On Tuesday, February 29th, dad was worried about how the Model T was going to be able to navigate the drifts for the three-mile trip to Lime Rock. At the Old Brown Table, Charles, his dad, provided wise counsel to his nervous son to forget the car and instead concentrate on the horse. After all, they had a brand-new sleigh and a horse, which could easily make the trip, albeit the blowing snow and high drifts.

So early on Wednesday morning, March 1st, Dad harnessed up the horse to the sleigh and readied for the three-mile trip. Dad, with his parents, Charles and Mary, made the trip without any problem, although they had to navigate through a few farmers' fields. The sleigh was even more romantic than the Model T since the bells on the horse's harness announced wedding bells to and from the church on that cold winter day, a day well remembered throughout the 47 years of their marriage. By the way, the Old Brown Table remembered as well.

LRGN: 3-1-1916.

"For the Lord is good;
His steadfast love endures forever,
And his faithfulness to all generations."
Psalm 100:5

Chapter Two

1920 to 1930 Old Brown Table Tales

Donald Woodward Airport Opening

After several weeks of rumors, it was formally announced in the May 2, 1928 edition of the Le Roy Gazette News that Donald Woodward would start construction of an airport on his farm east of the village. Donald was the son of Orator F. and Cora Talmadge Woodward, the founders of the Jell-O Company. He was a man of many talents and early in life found Kemp & Lane Inc to continue the manufacture of medicines produced originally by his father.

The airport would have two runways, one running north and south, and the other running east and west, allowing takeoff regardless of the wind direction. There would also be a hanger with classrooms, repair rooms, and a tower for control of aircraft. The article noted that Woodward owned four aircraft, including a Fairchild monoplane that he bought at Miami recently. His private pilot, Captain Russell Holderman, who served in World War I, would manage the airport and provide personal instructions to interested airmen.

There was a buzz of excited conversation around the Old Brown Table that Spring evening as to what effect this would have on the future of the town. The excitement was in the air, and town people wondered if this could transform Le Roy into a city larger than Batavia or Rochester. After all, Le Roy was blessed with several industries like the Jell-O, Lapp Insulator, and Union Steelchest. The author's brother, eleven-year-old Frank, was very excited since, as a young boy, he was interested in all types of flying machines like airplanes and flying dirigibles. He soon would develop an interest in becoming an aeronautical engineer.

As the construction commenced, it became evident that this was no ordinary airport of the time but far in advance of that seen in small or large cities. Airports at that time primarily consisted of dirt runways and wood barns for hangers compared to the Woodward airport with concrete runways and hanger. Later in mid-1930, a baseball field and miniature golf were added across from the airport, and a large restaurant on East Main road was opened in the Woodward barn making this a local community entertainment center.

Frank with His Homemade Airplane

Before the airport opening, it was announced that the aviation school, D. W. Flying Service would start with ten students from Buffalo, Rochester, and New York and was receiving applications almost daily.

News of the airport spread fast, and on October 12 – 14, the airport was formally opened with an impressive 75 planes participating. The September 26 edition of the Le Roy Gazette News reported that the event would be covered by leading film news organizations such as the Fox Film Company, the Pathe Company, and the International Newsreel. The town of Le Roy was now on the map for the nation to notice. On Friday, the outstanding event was the dedication address by Clarence M. Young of Washington, Director of Aeronautics Department of Commerce. He said, "Seldom does one man do so much for aviation as has been done here. Le Roy's airport is the envy and will be the envy for some time to come from many cities and communities having municipal airports. Donald Woodward is to be commended not only for what he has done for Le Roy and this territory but what he has done to promote aviation. This airport is the finest privately-owned airport in which the Department of Commerce has any knowledge. I know of no more fitting words with which to dedicate this fine airport than to the travelers of air and to those who would learn to fly."

On Saturday, airmail service was started for the first time in Le Roy with a plane carrying mail pouches left at 3:00 pm flying to the Britton field in Rochester. Many Le Royans and businesses filled the bags with airmail stamped letters anticipating them to be collector's items in years to come. An exhibition flight of Navy planes and pilots was provided, followed on Sunday with Army planes. The Le Roy High School band highlighted all of this at 11:00 am proudly showing their new uniforms.

Donald Woodward Airport LRHS

Even the Blue Bus Lines got in on the act announcing that the D. W. Airport would be an official stop, and the name was changed on the tickets from the Crusher Road to Le Roy Airport. Arrangements were also being made whereby tickets would be sold to any point in the country at the bus company ticket offices. A passenger in Buffalo or Rochester who wanted to fly to any location could purchase a through ticket at the point where he boarded the bus, would be taken to the Le Roy airport, and transferred to the air transportation line. Now that is 20th Century progress.

The Le Roy Gazette News reported, "The Sunday Assemblage Was the Largest in History for Genesee County" estimated at 75000. Since most people arrived by automobile, the highways were jammed bumper-to-bumper east and west for five miles. Many people abandoned their cars after waiting in traffic for hours and walked across fields to the airport. The New York State Police said this was one of the largest traffic jams they had ever witnessed, estimating the arrival of around 9000 cars.

On Sunday, the program opened when the 54th Regimental Band of Rochester played its rendition of "America." At 12:25 pm the formation of 75 planes was begun, lead with the Fairchild piloted by

Capt. Holderman. The Friendship, recently purchased by Don Woodward, circled Le Roy as the other planes were taking to the air to join the formation setting their compass to Rochester. The Friendship orange body glistening in the sun recently made the famed trans-Atlantic crossing just a few months earlier with Amelia Earhart as a passenger. The fleet of planes passed over the southern edge of Rochester turned at East Rochester and came back directly over the center of the city, arriving at the Don Woodward airport at 1:15 pm.

Later in the afternoon, four race events were run, and the planes provided many thrills for the crowd as they roared over a 12-mile course. A comedy flying team was enjoyable when the pilot flew around the course once, landing to a mark on the field, after which his mechanic or passenger ran 100 yards and consumed a large dish of Jell-O returning to the plane, which made another circle around the course. Needless to say, the winner was full of Jell-O, but what flavor? The event was followed by the parachute contest where jumpers were flown over the field in planes throwing themselves from the wings. They would then maneuver their parachutes to get as close to a large circle in the field. Some dropped several hundred feet before opening their chute, giving the crowd a thrill.

To the crowd's surprise, all events were performed without incident, remarkable since aviation was still in its infancy, and planes and pilots were still in the experimental phase relying on the most basic instruments and training. However, within one day after the opening, the airport did witness a plane crash. Navy Lieutenant Daniel T. Tomlinson was scheduled to give a stunt flight on Friday, but headwinds and poor visibility made it impossible for him to arrive on schedule. The Le Roy Gazette News reported on October 18, 1928, that he was flying from Long Beach, CA, and bucked thunderstorms nearly every day and landed the plane about every 250 miles to refuel. Tomlinson was the local hero since he was the son of Mr. and Mrs. D. W. Tomlinson of Batavia. On Monday, around 4:30 pm, just missing the airport opening by one day, he circled the D. W. Airport and was about to make a landing when the motor went dead, and the wind sent the plane into a wing slip from which it was impossible to recover. The landing gear of the Jenny bi-plane was taken out, and the wings were severely damaged. Lieutenant Tomlinson suffered a cracked jaw, and four of his teeth were knocked out. He was taken to the Batavia hospital for treatment by a dental surgeon and returned to his home in Batavia later in the evening. Officials at the airport said the accident would not have occurred if the lieutenant, leader of the "Sea Hawks," world's most outstanding formation stunt flyers, had been piloting a modern plane with a powerful motor. Only skillful handling of the old Curtiss "Jenny" prevented the flyer from more severe injury. Indeed, the Navy was far behind in possessing modern airplanes, which held the case until the start of WW II, several years later.

Well, the Old Brown Table heard several conversations in the fall of 1928 about the many new aspects of aviation leading up to the opening of the D. W. Airport. The entire family attended the opening on Saturday, October 13, and became frustrated when it seemed to take forever to reach the airport parking lot. The outstanding flying program made the delay well worth the wait as planes filled the sky with roaring engines passing over from every direction. On Sunday, the sky was filled with quite a variety of aircraft, which could be seen from the homestead on Warsaw road throughout the day. Indeed, Le Roy had made a quantum leap in history with the arrival of this advanced airport, and it was the inspiration to many enthusiasts for years to come.

LRGN: 5-2-1928; 9-12-1928; 10-17-1928.

1929 Year of Activity for D. W. Airport

There was no end of excitement at the D. W. Airport in the year following the Fall 1928 opening. Even though the new airport had been open for less than a year, the activity continued at a relentless pace with visiting dignitaries, new style airplanes, dirigibles, and the thrilling airplane races. The Old Brown Table was buzzing in conversation almost every week with current events at the airport. This was the end of the "Roaring Twenties," but it was just the beginning of a new era for the town of Le Roy.

The year started with the famous aviatrix Amelia Earhart on her visit on January 30, 1929, followed shortly afterward on February 5 with a Lindberg plane that was on its way to being delivered to Col. Charles Lindberg in New York City. The Sikorski amphibian plane, flown by pilot Walgren, was scheduled to be flown by Col. Lindberg to inaugurate the new Central America and Panama airmail route. Pilot Walgren was forced to land at the Le Roy port due to unfavorable weather and, after spending two days, became very impatient with the weather conditions. To the surprise of airport officials, he was so impatient he took off the next day in a snowstorm to deliver the plane to Lindberg in New York city. Pilots in the 1920s primarily flew by sight with the compass being the main instrument and would rarely fly at night or in poor weather conditions.

On February 13, Russ Holderman, manager of the D. W. Flying Service, joined a fleet of planes taking off from Miami to search for Col. Charles Lindberg, who was late on his return from the Central and South America airmail trip. During the search he discovered a plane in distress drifting off Long Key and upon landing with his Leoning amphibian took off the pilot and two passengers taking them to Miami. At this time, Holderman was arranging the opening of the D. W. Flying Service school of aeronautics on April 1. The school would offer courses in flying, navigation, and shop work, including a fifty-hour class in practical aviation along with instruction on the handling of the tri-motored "Friendship." All of this activity did not miss the attention of my brother Frank who at the age of 12 was already developing a keen interest in aeronautics, which usually resulted in many questions raised at the Old Brown Table.

Coincident at this time was the purchase by Kemp & Lane, a Donald Woodward business, of the Philadelphia company S. B. Goff & Sons. The company manufactured fourteen different proprietary articles, among which are Goff's Cough Syrup, Goff's Worm Syrup, Goff's Bitters, Hera Tonic and Herbitol Tonic. Also, the business included Goff's Atlantic City Salt Water Taffy, which had become widely distributed on the Eastern seaboard. After S. B. Goff & Sons was purchased in 1927, he bought the Orangeine Company in Chicago and moved it to Le Roy.

Also, at this time, the Woodward Memorial Library was in the planning phase. At one of the largest special school meetings, 400 Le Royans gathered in Ingham Hall at the high school building to voice their acceptance of the gifted library. The library was given to Le Roy by Ernest L. Woodward, O. Frank Woodward, Mrs. John Vietor, Donald Woodward, and Mrs. Helen Wilmsen in memory of their parents, the late Orator F. Woodward and Cora Talmadge Woodward.

Superintendent of Schools, Edward W. Spry, gave an address describing the new library in detail and that it would serve both village and school life. He gave recognition to Ernest Woodward in particular for his thoughtfulness and involvement for the use of the stone in the present Art College, which will now be torn down and used in the construction of the library.

The D. W. Airport made history again on May 11 when aerial golf would be played for the first time in Western New York as a result of a challenge issued by Russell Holderman and Edward M. Perkins to Otto Enderton and G. Roy McHardy. Aerial golf is played when the pilot flies over the green and drops a ball from the air as close to the green as he can manage following which the ground golfer plays it into the cup. There were to be a number of aerial golf games at the airport during the summer when prizes were offered that attracted pilots and golfers from Buffalo, Rochester, Syracuse and other places. However, that week the weather did not cooperate with a mean temperature of 49 Deg-F and rain almost every day. The weather made it very difficult for pilots and passengers to obtain their training during daylight hours, but on May 11, the weather cleared, and the aerial golf game went off as planned. However, the weather spoiled a west coast trip for Manager and Mrs. Russell W. Holderman when a low ceiling, adverse winds, and fog caused them to abandon the attempt at Indianapolis and return to Le Roy Monday. They had left the D. W. Airport Saturday at 11 am flying the Stearman with intentions to reach San Francisco in time to see Mr. and Mrs. Donald Woodward before they went on their honeymoon to Hawaii. In the meantime, the airport continued to attract several visitors, one of which was Wm. Sargent of the Department of Commerce flying a Travelair from Curtiss Field, Long Island. Le Roy was indeed on the national map just the same as a major city.

July 4th weekend was a buzz of activity at the airport leading off with a 30-mile race among pilots of the D-W Flying Service who challenged each other as to the speed of their Waco airplanes that are used in training. On Thursday, July 4, Lady Heath, the famous English aviatrix, landed at the airport and motored to Batavia, where she spoke on the Chautaugua program. The next day at the airport, she talked to Captain Holderman, telling him, "I have seen many airports throughout the world, and so far as I know, this airport is the finest private airport in the world." Captain Holderman said he had met Lady Heath in Miami, where both were entered in a race at the opening of the airport there. He said she is a splendid pilot and has done much to advance aviation. Later that day, there were high winds, so passenger flying was canceled, but Holderman demonstrated an unusual feat when he put his plane into the wind over the field, whereby the aircraft remained stationary. Upon reducing the speed, his plane moved backward to the amazement of the crowd. One week later, Capt. Holderman won a 25-mile race in Bradford, PA, winning a prize of $500 ($7500 in 2020 dollars). Not bad for a single race!

In August, the D. W. Flying Service offered flying instruction to the State Troopers at Troop A in Batavia with the forethought that flying troopers will be necessary within the decade. A glider was also purchased since gliding a plane with no power was becoming increasingly popular. On August 17, the St. Louis Robin, a Curtiss airplane which set a world's endurance record of more than 420 hours, landed at the airport for a short visit. The famous pilots, Red Jackson and Forest O'Brine, were accompanied by officials of the Curtiss company who were traveling in a Ford tri-motored monoplane. They were in agreement without doubt the Le Roy airport was the finest in the nation. Jackson and O'Brine flew from Le Roy to Syracuse where a mishap occurred with the Robin upon landing. O'Brine, when landing, the plane caught his heel in

Goodyear Blimp at DW Airport

a cleat, jamming the controls, and in the resulting crash, the landing gear and fabric of the right-wing were damaged.

The Old Brown Table listened to excited chatter on Wednesday, August 28, when it was heard the giant dirigible Los Angeles could be sighted over Le Roy around 3:30 pm. The dirigible was on the way to the Cleveland Air Races, where the German dirigible Graf Zepplin would be present. The Graf Zepplin would also be visible when it travels from Cleveland to Lakehurst, NJ. These airships were indeed impressive due to their size, the Graf Zepplin measuring around 700 feet long, a diameter of 100 feet, a crew of 36, and a passenger capacity of 20. The gas volume was 2,600,000 cu ft of hydrogen and 1,100,000 cu ft of Blau gas. The powerplant was five Maybach VLII V012 piston engines, 550 hp each. It could reach a speed of 80 mph and had a range of 6200 miles, far exceeding any other conceivable aircraft. Again, the Le Roy D. W. Airport was attracting aeronautical marvels for the local town to see.

As fall approached, more dignitaries arrived at D. W. with the arrival of the Columbia airplane owned by Charles Levine, which made a trans-Atlantic flight earlier by pilots Roger C. Williams and Captain Louis A. Yancey flying the Atlantic into Rome, Italy. At about the same time, it was announced that Donald Woodward had purchased the 126 ft ocean yacht Murdona. The vessel was powered by two 250 Hp Winton diesel engines providing a speed of 13 knots per hour and a cruising range of 3000 miles. Plans were made for a two-week cruise along the New England coast, followed by a cruise to Florida and the Caribbean.

Le Roy was put on the map again October 10 when Assistant Secretary of War in charge of aviation, F. Trubee Davison, visited the D. W. Airport along with Lieutenant Maitland, a pilot who flew a record flight to Honolulu on July 28, 1927. A small company of Le Royans was invited for breakfast with Secretary Davison at the home of Mr. and Mrs. Russell Holderman.

The second annual air meet at D. W. was held on October 11-13, 1929, Friday through Sunday, and drew thousands of spectators braving an average temperature of 51 Deg-F and a few short rain showers. The thrills and excitement started on Friday with 3000 taking advantage of free admission, Saturday with 5000 spectators, and Sunday with an estimated 12000. The attendance did not match last year's attendance of 50000 due to a fear of traffic jams and the 50 cent ($7.50 in 2020 dollars) admission charged on Saturday and Sunday. Nevertheless, there was an excellent response of aircraft, which at one point numbered 68 on the field. The eight air races, a few up to 60 miles in length, were exciting with several close finishes with a total of $4750 ($71381 in 2020 dollars) of prizes. The stunt flying was exceptional, and special features such as parachute drops, glider contests, and skywriting were performed right on schedule. The Le Roy Business Association presented the winners of the races with a travel clock and a gold-plated Gillette "Tuckaway" safety razor engraved with the date of the meet. Don Woodward arrived at the meet on Friday afternoon from Boston via a tri-motored Ford airliner, which he chartered for the trip, accompanied by Mrs. Woodward and her two brothers. Many dignitaries attended the meet with 300 enjoying a clambake supper in the hanger on Saturday evening.

The 1929 year of aviation activity concluded with Capt. Russell Holderman, vice president and general manager of the D. W. Flying Service having a narrow escape at the Perry, NY, air meet. Holderman was participating in a race when the engine of his Challenger plane blew up, sending smoke, oil, and debris into the air. Holderman said the whole front section of the engine and propeller fell off, causing the cowling to hit the wing, causing the plane to swing sharply to the left. With his experience and skill, he was able to maintain control even though he was only 200 ft in altitude. He was able to make a pancake landing and escaped injury. However, a parachutist, Amos McGuire of Rochester, was not so lucky when his chute did not open and was killed instantly.

The Old Brown Table, throughout 1929, always heard an exciting conversation about the D. W. Airport activities with the family attending events whenever possible. However, in late October, there occurred the famous Wall Street Crash of 1929, which initiated the start of the Great Depression with many bank failures and corporate bankruptcies. It was truly a year to be remembered.

LRGN: 9-5-1928; 2-6,20,27-1929; 5-1,15-1929; 6-19-1929; 7-3,10,17-1929; 8-14,21,28-1929; 9-4-1929; 10-16-1929; 11-13-1929.

Amelia Earhart Is Coming To Le Roy

Le Roy was astounded in January 1929 when it was announced in the Le Roy Gazette that the aviatrix Amelia Earhart would be coming to make an appearance at the D. W. Airport. She was world-famous since she was the first woman to cross the Atlantic Ocean on June 17, 1928, in the large Friendship three-engine airplane.

There was a lot of conversation at the Old Brown Table on the evening of January 23 that the remarkable Amelia would be in Le Roy for all to witness. There was no question the family would attend regardless of the cold January weather.

Amelia developed an interest in aviation ever since her father paid $10 for her to fly with Frank Hawks on a 10-minute flight from Long Beach on December 28, 1920. She said, "By the time I had got two or three hundred feet off the ground, I knew I had to fly." From that point on she worked at various jobs to save $1000 for flying lessons. In the summer of 1921, Earhart purchased a secondhand bright yellow Kinner Airster biplane she nicknamed "The Canary", which she flew to an altitude of 14000 feet setting a world record for a female pilot. On May 15, 1923 she became the 16th woman in the country to be issued a pilot's license.

In 1927 aviation history was marked in the solo flight of Charles Lindberg across the Atlantic Ocean. At the same time British Lady Guest expressed an interest in being the first woman to fly or be flown across the Atlantic. After learning the perils and high risk of such a trip she offered to sponsor the project and find another girl with the right image. Since Earhart was somewhat known from her previous flights, a call was received from Capt. Hilton H. Railey, who asked her, "Would you like to fly the Atlantic?" The project coordinators, which included publisher and publicist George P. Putnam, interviewed Earhart and asked her to accompany pilot Wilmer Stultz and co-pilot/mechanic Louis Gordon on the Atlantic flight as a passenger with the responsibility to keep the flight log.

The team left Trepassey Harbor, Newfoundland on June 17, 1928 in a Fokker F. Vilb with pontoons providing ability to take off and land on water. The flight was highly successful and took 20 hours and 40 minutes landing in South Wales. Most of the flight was on instruments and Earhart had no training for instrument flying so she did not pilot the aircraft. She said upon landing, "Stultz did all the flying—had too. I was just baggage, like a sack of potatoes." Regardless the newsreels instantly made Amelia a national hero as the "First Woman to Fly the Atlantic." Just over a month later, on July 27, Donald Woodward purchased the Friendship from Lady Guest of London, England, who sponsored the trans-Atlantic flight. The plane was then shipped to New York, where it was wholly reconditioned before coming to Le Roy. Changes were made in the addition of windows to the cabin and the replacement of pontoons with landing gear.

On a cold winter day in upstate New York with temperatures barely reaching 41 Deg-F, Amelia arrived in Rochester, NY, and was described by reporters as a "slender, fair-haired girl in a smart black suit with a varicolored scarf, blue hat and wearing a corsage." She attended the Lady's Day luncheon of the Rochester Ad Club before motoring to Le Roy, accompanied by members of the Rochester reception committee. Upon arrival at the D. W. Airport at around 2:45 pm she was met by a large Le Roy crowd. Also, she was introduced to a local committee composed of Le Roy dignitaries, including a personal friend, Nat Bowle, who was the architect for the airport associated with the builder, John H. Pike & Son.

Amelia Earhart LRHS

She was escorted on a tour of the airport seeing the offices, the observation tower, the student classrooms, repair shop, and the hanger, which held the famous tri-motored Fokker monoplane in which she made the historic flight. Miss Earhart complied with the requests of press reporters and photographers. She was kept busy posing for pictures in various groups beside the Friendship and autographed several letters to be forwarded to members of the Woodward family. The Le Roy crowd greeted her warmly with sustained applause.

After a tea at the home of Miss Elizabeth Wells with twenty guests present, she returned to Rochester. She was a guest at a dinner given by the directors of the Rochester Automobile Dealers Association then attending the automobile show at Edgerton Park.

Indeed, a memorable day conversed at the Old Brown Table since Miss Earhart was a world-famous aviatrix and later went on to set several aviation records. Unfortunately, in attempting an around the world flight in 1937, Earhart and her navigator Fred Noonan disappeared over the central Pacific Ocean near Howland Island.

Several attempts to find them or their plane have been made over the years with tragically no success.

LRGN: 1-23-29; 1-30-29; Wikipedia Amelia Earhart.

Ford Model T Wreck

On April 23, 1929, the Old Brown Table witnessed sad news on serious injuries that were received by five-year-old Mary Johanna Brown in a car accident occurring that evening. The parent's Jack and Nellie Brown with their daughter Mary were traveling in the 1916 Ford Model T to visit some friends in Le Roy. Jack had stopped at the red flasher at the corner of North and South streets when they were struck by a car traveling west on Main Street crossing in front of them through the signal. The impact drove Jack's Model T into the southwest corner of the intersection. Nellie was cut on the hand, and Mary was cut about the head and sustained a fracture of her skull. Dr. T. Murray Steele immediately took them both to St. Jerome's Hospital in Batavia.

Henry Ford Model T

John M. Maloy of Le Roy, the driver of the other car, sustained injuries to his teeth and lip and was attended to by Dr. G. Henry Knoll. Jack Brown had Maloy arrested on a charge of reckless driving following the accident. Maloy deposited $50 for his appearance in court at 10 am the next morning when the case was adjourned to May 8, 1929.

The 1916 Model T windshield was ordinary window glass, which would shatter on impact into several shards of glass cutting anyone in its path. There was a lawsuit, Pane vs. Ford, in 1917, charging Ford to not using proper glass and, as a result causing severe injury to the auto's occupants. The case was decided against Pane in that he was only injured as a result of his reckless driving. In 1919 however, Henry Ford solved the problem of windshields shattering, causing serious injury by using the new French technology of glass laminating. Windshields made using this process were two layers of glass with a cellulose inner layer. This inner layer held the glass together when it fractured. Between 1919 and 1929, Ford ordered the use of laminated glass on all of his vehicles. But this was too late for the 1916 Model T.

As a result of the injury, Mary did have a scar on her forehead for the rest of her life. Another consequence of the accident could have also had a lasting effect. Jack was carrying in the car a gallon of homemade wine. Since he had a large vineyard used primarily to raise and sell Concord grapes, he would make red wine from the waste grapes. He would serve the wine at the homestead for guests and would deliver the wine as a goodwill gift to relatives. Unfortunately, this was during the Prohibition era, where it was unlawful to sell or transport intoxicating beverages. When the glass gallon jug of wine broke as a result of the accident impact, it was evident Jack was transporting wine. John Maloy made that fact known to the police who charged Jack, and he was ordered to a hearing before the Le Roy magistrate. Jack determined he needed a lawyer, so he asked his brother-in-law, Bill Ireland if he could lend assistance with a lawyer from his company. Ireland was the sales manager for the Todd Company in Rochester, which was a nationwide office equipment company. The lawyer represented Jack at the hearing, and the town magistrate was no match for the argument presented. That evening The Old Brown Table heard the good news that the charges were dropped. Jack also learned a lesson never to transport wine again.

LRGN: 4-24-29.

Golden Celebration at the Old Brown Table

August 22, 1923, marked a day of celebration at the homestead of Charles and Mary Baroncini Brown. It was their golden wedding anniversary attended by their immediate family members.

Sons and daughters arrived from Buffalo and as far away as Erie, PA, to be with their Dad and Mom on this great occasion. Those present included from Le Roy, Mr. and Mrs. Jack Brown and family, Mr. and Mrs. John Brown and Mrs. John Stefani. From Buffalo, Mr. and Mrs. Charles Sr. Brown and family, Mr. and Mrs. Anthony Marr and family, Mr. and Mrs. Melvin Rossi, Miss Mabel Marr and from Erie, PA, Mr. and Mrs. William Ireland. In the evening at the Old Brown Table, Charles was presented with a gold watch, and Mary was presented with six five-dollar gold pieces.

Brown-Baroncini Reunion 1923

They all stayed for a few days enjoying good food and endless conversation catching up on family events. They also enjoyed playing cards, and the men went hunting and fishing in the surrounding fields. Since there weren't sufficient accommodations in the farmhouse, the men slept in the haymow on the upper floor of the red barn with the cow and horse below.

Charles Baroncini Brown proudly showed off his new Ford Model T touring car, which he had purchased on April 12, 1922, from E. Townsend & Son. There were no side windows but only canvas curtains that would sort of keep out the cold winter wind. However, the car was not used in the cold, snowy New York State winters due to the poor road conditions, so it was placed up on blocks in the red barn. The reliable horse and buggy, along with the sleigh, were the primary transportation means during the winter season.

LRGN: 4-12-1922; 8-22-1923.

Oh Cow, Where Art Thou?

My Grandpa & Grandma Baroncini Brown lived in the foothills of the Alps in Northern Italy during the late 1800s before immigrating to America around 1882. Around 1903 they moved from renting a small apartment in Buffalo to establishing the farm and farmhouse on Route 19 called Warsaw Road. This would be the first chance Grandpa could practice his farming talents in the USA. He soon planted apple, pear, and peach trees, and with pride, he grafted into the apple tree three different kinds of apples. Then he planted a large raspberry patch and a large garden, which provided adequate produce for sale to the grocery stores in Le Roy. He was assisted in all of these endeavors by his young son Jacob, my father who was commonly called Jack. Jack supplemented the farm income by working as a molder at the Le Roy Plow Company.

Grandpa's Betsy

To fulfill a country diet Grandpa purchased a horse, a cow, chickens and pigs. The horse was used for travel to town along with tilling the fields and the cow became the source of milk year-round. Now the cow called Betsy was housed in the barn during the winter but was allowed to graze during the summer in the adjoining lot next to the barn. However, since the pasture was not fenced Betsy would be tied with a long rope providing plenty of grazing room.

One day the line came loose, and the Betsy started to enjoy more of the pasture moving toward Cole Road. Betsy being an adventurous cow who wanted to see the world took a journey to the B&O railroad tracks and followed the tracks south. In late afternoon Grandpa went to milk the cow but it could not be found at the rope or anywhere else on the farm property. At about that time Jack returned home from work and joined Grandpa in the search. They talked to Andy Meehan across the street who had not seen the cow but he kindly joined the search as well since a cow was a valuable asset that you would not give up on easily. Was it possible the cow was kidnapped? That seemed unlikely since there were no reports of cow kidnapping in the Le Roy area. It was now getting dark so the search was suspended until the next morning.

Very early in the morning after searching to the east and then to the south Betsy was not found at the Johnson milk farm as would be expected. The next search area was to the south along the B&O railroad tracks crossing Cole road, which brought speculation that the cow would likely be struck by a train since cows do not have a high enough IQ to avoid trains. Further south along the railroad track the party searched until Beaver Meadow came into view. Now Beaver Meadow was a rather large swamp with an area of about 30 acres filled with cattails. It wasn't long before Betsy was found in the swamp not far from the railroad. Betsy was mired in muck up her belly and could not move. Grandpa went back to the farm and brought the horse back to the swamp with a long rope. Betsy was roped around the front quarters and the horse pulled with sufficient force to move Betsy from the swamp.

Betsy could hardly make it back to the farm about two miles distant and after laying down in the barn taking a long-awaited rest, Grandpa tried to milk her but she would not stand for it after the swamp ordeal. Later in the evening Grandpa tried to milk her again but no milk was produced, not even a drop. Now, this caused some concern since Betsy always gave an adequate supply of milk in the early morning and late afternoon. Well for the next several days Grandpa tried again and again but no milk came forth. He then realized that since Betsy was not milked on the day she disappeared, and the day following her milk-producing glans had been severely damaged.

The Old Brown Table now heard talk about what to do with Betsy. Do you eat her and that of course was unacceptable since she was part of the family after several years of loyalty? So, Betsy was put up for sale and soon a buyer purchased Betsy. Now Grandpa thought he would never be able to sell a dry milk cow so the buyer was never told. Betsy's last moo was, "Buyer Beware of Straying Cows!"

What, Talking Movies?

Silent movies were the norm in the early 1920s with sound provided by a theatre piano or organ with the audience reading the on-screen script to keep pace with the story. The actor would use facial expressions and body language to convey a story to the audience. Then in late 1929 at about the time of the stock market crash on Wall Street, talking movies made their debut in Le Roy almost timed perfectly to calm the fears of Le Roy over the pending doom of investments and banks.

The movie picture business had been in an unsettled state during the past year as various systems to provide talking movies were tried with unsatisfactory results. Some of the earlier systems recorded sound on discs, which most of the time was out of sync with the picture resulting in many dissatisfied customers. The sound design of the Cinephone is part of the film itself, offering perfect synchronization.

The exciting news in Le Roy appeared in the Le Roy Gazette on October 23, 1929, with the front-page headline, "Sound Movies to Open Here Sunday, New Equipment at the Family Theatre." The manager, Ralph Blouvet, announced they would offer to the people of Le Roy, "The Sophomore" featuring the dancing singing, petite Sally O'Neil in a college play that ripples with life and interest. He said, "Mechanics have been in Le Roy the past two weeks making installation of the Power's Cinephone, the outstanding device today for projecting the picture on the screen and filling the auditorium with the voices and music of the players". The article went on to say that the moving picture business has been in a most unsettled state during the past two years resulting in managers not knowing what was to be the outcome of the talking movie. At first, the sound was recorded on discs, which was usually out of sync with the picture. Then came the incredible invention called Cinephone, where the sound is part of the film itself since it synchronizes perfectly with the picture.

Just a few months later, on March 5, 1930, the Family Theatre advertised the "Shannons of Broadway," a comedy team and Will Rogers in "They Had to See Paris." Will Rogers, at that time, was the most publicized man in the country with over two hundred newspapers carrying his daily message. Dinner at the Old Brown table was accompanied by conversation and laughter over the scenes from these movies. What a delight from the bad economic news over the radio and newspapers on bank closings and companies going into bankruptcy.

The entertainment was reasonable in price, and the competition was minimal before television emerged in the late 1940s. Seeing a movie or the usual double feature was common, especially on Saturday or Sunday. The usual routine was a movie followed by a short trip to Ellis or Tountas Ice Cream Shoppe, and don't forget the ice cream counter at Cut-Rate Drugs. Upon arrival home, the Old Brown Table would hear comments and discussion on the movie(s) just viewed. Sometimes it was a terrific show, and sometimes it was a bomb, but that did not hold adults and children alike from attending whenever they were able.

On October 12, 1932, the Le Roy Theatre opened by the owner Ralph E. Blouvet presenting the latest film, "Rebecca of Sunnybrook Farm." A Le Roy Gazette article stated, "No better selection could have been made for the opening of the village theatre than the sweet, wholesome story, which has gained fame both in book form and on the legitimate stage." The main attraction was accompanied with the comedy, "County Hospital," a Mickey Mouse cartoon, Metro News Events, and the "Musical Magic Carpet," where you could sing with the music following the words on the screen with the bouncing ball. Now that's Entertainment! Recognition of the opening as constituting a desirable addition in community life was Mayor John P. Gleason and Sidney D. O'Shea' president of the Le Roy Business Association. All of Le Roy had taken a keen interest in the building of the theatre considered most attractive due to the credit of the local architect

Charles I. Cromwell. The foyer was spacious with auditorium seating of 340 seats and a balcony of 131 seats, fifty of which are lodge seats, the most desired in the theatre. The Old Brown Table sure heard many favorable comments on this newest addition to the village of Le Roy.

The Brown family, along with thousands across America, were now to become dedicated fans of the talking pictures for years to come. Ralph E. Blouvet was to be congratulated for using the latest technology for the benefit of the Le Roy community.

LRGN: 10-23-29; 11-27-29.

> "Bless the Lord, O my soul,
> And all that is within me,
> Bless his holy name!"
> Psalm 103:1

Chapter Three

1930 to 1940 Old Brown Table Tales

Come Play with Me

We would entertain many visitors to our home in Le Roy, which turned out to be primarily relatives on my mother's side of the family. We would usually gather in the kitchen around the Old Brown Table, and if it were a larger group than the kitchen could comfortably hold, the group would divide with the women in the living room and the men in the kitchen.

I remember as a young four-year-old boy, we had a visit one day from a Spencerport, NY, family, that were relatives of my Uncle Bill and Aunt Francis Ireland. My Uncle Bill had two unmarried sisters and a dwarf brother. The dwarf brother named Floyd entered the kitchen with his two sisters, and I was immediately impressed with the size of his large head and tiny body. As my Dad and Mom exchanged light conversation with our guests, I gazed intently at Floyd and noticed that he did not join in on the conversation with the others.

Well, I thought this was the opportune time to entertain the dwarf Floyd. I went into my bedroom and gathered up a handful of toys and cheerfully brought them into the kitchen, noisily dropping them on the kitchen floor and kindly offered a toy to Floyd. Well, I expected Floyd to take the toy joyfully and, of course, play with me. To my utter surprise, everybody in the kitchen burst out with laughter. My Mom kindly informed me that Floyd was not a young boy like me but was a very mature adult no longer interested in toys. That was a shock and disappointment, but I was over it in a second, and though embarrassed went on, amusing myself with my toys.

Frank, You Captured My Clothesline

Mom had a routine when she washed the family's clothes. In the back kitchen, there was the Maytag washer that seemed to last forever. Whenever it broke down, a part was replaced, and it got a reprieve on life. She would wash clothes first with Fels Naphtha soap, which had a very distinct strong fragrance. Then she would use the roll ringer to squeeze out the wash water and send the clothes into the concrete tub filled with cold rainwater. The rinsed clothes were placed through the roller again with a final roll into the basket. The clothes were then taken outside to hang on the clothesline.

In the winter, she would hang the clothes on a line on the front porch, and when she would bring the clothes inside, they would be frozen stiff as a board. There was a wooden clothes rack over the four-foot furnace register in the living room where the clothes would finally dry. Of course, in the summer, the clothes would be brought outside and hung on four 20-foot-long lines between two T-posts. If there were more clothes than usual, there was a line that was close to the driveway turn-around where cars would back before heading out the driveway to Route 19, Warsaw Road.

1936 Lasalle

In the late 1930s, her son Frank bought a used 1936 four-door Lasalle, which was the forerunner of today's Cadillac. It was a

31

beautiful car with a powerful straight eight-cylinder engine and displayed a very smooth ride. One day when Frank was going into town, he backed up into the turn-around, and the trunk handle hooked onto Mom's clothesline. When he pulled forward, he took the line clothes and all and sped out the drive to downtown Le Roy about two miles north.

When Frank drove his Lasalle proudly down Main Street, he couldn't help but notice that he was getting seen much more than the Lasalle deserved. He diagonal parked on Main Street and then made the horrible discovery. There were shirts, pants, dresses, and of course, underwear being dragged behind his beautiful Lasalle. Red-faced, he picked up the clothes as fast and inconspicuous as he could muster and placed them in the back seat.

On returning home, the Old Brown Table witnessed a direct exchange between Mom and Frank and guess which one was on the losing side. From that day on, Frank was very cautious when he reversed into the turn-around because that error was never to be made again. Just ask the Old Brown Table!

Slap on the Back

As a young child, did you like candy? I mean those fantastic chocolate bars like Hershey, Mars, Almond Joy, Candy Cigarettes, Dots, just to name a few. One candy that was my favorite was hard candy called Jawbreakers. I don't know how my teeth took the punishment, but I loved to suck on them, and the flavor would last much longer than the chocolate candy bar.

One day I was in the kitchen by the Old Brown Table sucking on a Jawbreaker when all of a sudden, it somehow went down my throat, and I realized I could not get my breath. I made a terrible noise, not understanding what was happening but in horror realized that I was choking. Fortunately, my sister Eleanor was in the kitchen, and while yelling, he's choking, she ran over to me and gave me a hard slap on my back. I lunged forward with my mouth open, and the Jawbreaker became dislodged from my windpipe and shot across The Old Brown

Table with incredible force hitting the wall on the opposite side of the room. With relief, I could breathe again, although a bit terrified. I was forever grateful to my sister for the act of mercy she instinctively performed.

Later in life, I found out that the Jawbreaker could have gone down further in my windpipe, and that would have been the end of Billy at the age of five. Sadly, my sister Eleanor was not as fortunate because she choked to death while eating dinner in a nursing home many years later.

Sunday Noon Spaghetti Dinners

One of the traditions at the Old Brown Table was Sunday dinner with the family. These dinners were usually spaghetti and meatballs cooked by Mom and certainly enjoyed by all present. Mom was an excellent cook in whatever cuisine she would try. Sometimes she would surprise us with roast pork, fried chicken, roast beef, or turkey, all of which were delicious. After dinner, we would sit around the table discussing many issues of the day, usually with coffee and pie. She had her favorites like the Sunday noon dinner, but often during the week, she would choose a recipe from the newspaper or a favorite cookbook. She would cook primarily from memory because when you asked for the recipe, she would rattle it off and expect you to remember it.

The Sunday dinner usually included spaghetti accompanied with her homemade spaghetti sauce and, of course, homemade meatballs. The meatballs were freshly made just before dinner from hamburger mixed with chopped onion, garlic, and oregano. Then there were the homemade dinner rolls and real butter, never the artificial type. The salad would always accompany the meal. Usually, lettuce and tomatoes from the garden or in winter there would be squash, home-canned beets or corn. Then, of course, dessert, usually pineapple upside-down cake except when strawberries were in season. Strawberry shortcake with real whipped cream was always a favorite. Mom's pies were delicious. During the week, she would sit at the Old

Brown Table slicing apples, then standing, add sugar, cinnamon, and a little flour and mix. The grandchildren would ask for a few of those apple slices to taste. Then she would roll out the piecrust on a cutting board that was sprinkled with some flour on the Old Brown Table. The remarkable feat was that her piecrust was always in one piece, whether apple, cherry, or peach, baked perfectly on that old kitchen stove. The success must be attributed to Mom's love.

Now conversation at Sunday dinner was commonly on the political side. Dad would expound on the president and the economy, and being a Republican would down the Democratic view. When Dad and Mom lost their oldest son Frank in combat on June 8, 1944, Dad could only talk about the mistakes the politicians were making. President Franklin D. Roosevelt was the villain in those days, especially when he and Prime Minister Winston Churchill gave Stalin most of Eastern Europe. We would sit at the table after dessert and be a captive audience for Dad. My brother Al would sometimes offer a different point of view, which was met with a counterview from Dad. Both thought they were right, so there was always an ongoing argument. Mom would get up and leave the table, and the rest of us would look for the opportunity to do the same. The Old Brown Table heard many a hot argument in the '40s and '50s. The lesson I learned was to listen with patience and escape when you can. In time I would have my own opinion and view, which I would express to my children. Yes, at the Sunday dinner table.

The Head Hole

As a small boy playing outside was always an adventure, whether it was hot in the summer or cold and snowy in the winter. I always found something to do even though I did not have any playmates since we lived in the country. On a cold winter day, I would build a snowman or a snow cave, depending on the depth and quality of the snow. The winters in the late '40s were quite severe, with the event of several snowstorms depositing several feet of snow. The old farmhouse was not insulated, which produced long icicles some three to four feet long that would hang suspended from the gutters. They were a beautiful sight when the sun would shine and glisten from the frozen icicle. I made up a game of trying to pull off the longest icicle and then use it as a spear toward an imaginary target.

One day while engaged in this vital activity, I grabbed an icicle pulling it off when the icicle next to it came loose and struck me square on the top of my head. I reeled back in some pain and quite startled by the shock. I yelled out a scream and headed for the back door. I found my mom in the kitchen by the Old Brown Table, pulled off my stocking cap, and asked her to find the hole in my head. She, of course, laughed, but to soothe my nerves, she told me that I survived the icicle attack without a hole in my head. She then sat me down with hot cocoa and one of her homemade cookies, which of course, cured the hole in my head.

Well, from that day forward, I had more respect for those beautiful long icicles and let mother nature take care of their plight.

"I give thanks to you, O Lord my God, with my whole heart,
And I will glorify your name forever."
Psalm 86:12

Chapter Four

1940 To 1950 Old Brown Table Tales

Al Won a Farnsworth

Around 1950 there was excitement in the Brown family when gathered around the Old Brown Table. Al announced that he won a combination radio-phonograph at a raffle. He was attending dances at Silver Lake, and he bought a ticket for a raffle on a floor model Farnsworth AM/FM radio and phonograph. We were all excited when he picked up his prize and brought it home on a pickup truck. The hardwood cabinet was incredibly stylish with a lid that could be raised or lowered. Al proudly plugged it in and turned on the FM radio. The sound was significant coming from the front 12-inch speaker producing magnificent treble and base. We had a few 78 records at home, and we enjoyed what sounded like the philharmonic was right in our living room.

Al was not the only one that was blessed with a win. Just two years prior, when I was only seven years old, my Dad took me to a barber in Lime Rock. In the barbershop, there was a punchboard game. If you paid 25 cents, you could use a nail sized punch and push through one of the many small indentations. Out would come a small piece of paper with a number that you would match against a few prizes. My number was the prize of a table radio on the shelf. It was a Crosley AM radio that I was allowed to keep in my bedroom for my listening pleasure. Yes, it was the old tube-type since the solid-state transistor radio had not been invented yet.

Aunt Katies

Whenever I heard the name Aunt Katie, I felt a warm feeling in my childhood heart. Aunt Katie was disabled her entire life after she was injured as a three-year-old child when a heavy barrel fell on her. The doctor did not appropriately set her fractured hip, and this caused one leg to be about four inches shorter than the other. She used a crutch and a cane to aid her walking ability, and she did manage quite well.

During the summer vacation months, she would invite a cousin and me to her home in Mumford, NY, for a week. I enjoyed this immensely since she would always buy us candy at the local store, and on rare occasions, she would give me an old coin from her collection. Aunt Katie and Uncle Bob lived in a small house behind the Mumford post office. We would sleep in a small guest bedroom just off the living room decorated in a dark floral wallpaper. There was an upstairs with a low ceiling, which we were told to avoid, but we explored it anyway as would young adventurous kids.

Aunt Katie Kelly

Aunt Katie gave us the freedom to walk to the New York State Fish Hatchery, which was over the bridge spanning the B&O railroad with a small red brick train station behind the Springbrook Inn. We would watch the minnows in the canals at the fish hatchery, and no one ever told us as curious children to leave.

37

One day my cousin and I decided we would go fishing in the O-At-Ka Creek just a quarter-mile north of her home. We did not have fishing poles, so we cut two small branches from a bush and borrowed some string from Aunt Katie, who permitted us to fish after supper. Uncle Bob, who worked as a state highway worker, came home at the usual time, and after supper, we got ready for our great fishing expedition. Now we did not have any bait, but using our boyhood intellect, we found some in the kitchen.

Off we went with visions of bringing home a large fish for Aunt Katie to fry on that old stove in the kitchen. Her kitchen was quite primitive since there was a hand pump by the sink that drew water from the well outside, and she cooked on a wood-fired cast iron stove. But that never held her back from making delicious meals and, of course, fabulous cookies.

We arrived at the bank of the O-At-Ka creek by the highway bridge and found what we thought was an ideal fishing spot. We baited our hooks and cast our string line into the water. After a half-hour of no results, we saw two men with fishing poles, and tackle boxes cast their fishing line very close to the bridge. After a few minutes, one of the men yelled, "Hey, kids, what are you using as bait?" Well, we had no secrets, so we shouted back, "Flies." He yelled back, "What type of flies are you using?" With total innocents, we exclaimed, "Kitchen Flies!" after which the men burst out laughing. I then heard the other man say, "Joe, they will catch more fish than us."

We did not completely understand what all the laughter was about, but we left anyway since when you do not catch a fish within a half-hour, it is time to head home. A few days later, the Old Brown Table heard our story, and Dad and Mom laughed just like the men at the creek. We never understood what was so humorous!

Baby Woodchuck

One cold winter night, my brother Al brought into the farmhouse kitchen in his hand a tiny animal wrapped in a rag. It was the cutest little creature you could ever set eyes on, a baby woodchuck or as otherwise named a groundhog. Al found it in the red barn, and somehow it was separated from its mom. Since it looked hungry, I found a small doll baby bottle and filled it with milk. At the Old Brown Table, the little creature sucked away and drank his fill of farm milk until two bottles were consumed. He then went to sleep, and I prepared a nice warm bed of rags in a small cigar box.

I now had a wonderful pet much better than our cat "Blackie" since I did not see much of the cat in the winter because it was an outdoor cat. At that time, I was seeing a lot of Tarzan movies at the Le Roy Theatre and just loved the monkey Cheeta. I asked Mom for a monkey and was flatly denied. I thought what is wrong with a monkey because they were incredibly cute and did extraordinary things.

Well, that night, there was much joy around the Old Brown Table until it was time for me to go to bed. I had already made grandiose plans to take my newfound pet to bed with me. However, my Mom uttered those fateful words, "A woodchuck is not going to be in my house!" Despite my pleading, those were the final words, and the woodchuck had to be taken to the barn where it was found, but at least I was told it had a full stomach and a bed.

The next day when I awoke, I could not wait to see my new pet. My brother Al brought it in from the red barn, and to my horror, it did not move. Yes, the baby woodchuck succumbed to the cold and died that night with a full stomach. I was told the woodchuck probably died from pneumonia, but that did not help my grief. Of course, I was also informed the animal would never have survived captivity, but that is little consolation to a small boy wanting an animal friend.

It was only a year later in the spring of 1941 around the time of Easter that we had a visit from my Uncle Bill and Aunt Fran Ireland, who lived in Rochester at the time. When they entered the house and stopped at the Old Brown Table, I noticed that Uncle Bill had something in his pocket. I always admired Uncle Bill because he had an incredible sense of humor and could get you laughing by just looking at you with that silly smile on his face. Well, to my astonishment, he pulls a puppy from his pocket and hands it to me. Well, the first thing the puppy did was wee-wee on my hands and the floor. To a young boy around six, that did not matter as I brought my puppy outside, where I did not even notice it was cold and wet as most springs are around Easter in upper New York State.

I named the puppy "Pal," of course, where a long relationship developed between a boy and his dog. Pal would go everywhere with me around the farm and on long hikes through the surrounding forests and farmland. Always there except for some reason, I could not understand Pal would disappear for about two weeks, usually in the spring of the year. My Dad and I would take the car and go out hunting for Pal and would soon find him at a distant farm with other dogs. Pal would be in terrible shape, dirty, thin, and with a shameful appearance. Upon inquiring, my Dad could only explain at the Old Brown Table that Pal had a girlfriend he had to visit once a year. I never could understand why Pal would pick a girlfriend over me. Well, today I do!

Billy with His New Dog Pal

Black Hawk Was Here

When I was around 12 years old, I developed a keen interest in making things, which led me to build a shack in an ideal location at the Brown homestead on Warsaw road. Several hundred feet behind the house and red barn was a wooded area between the field and the B&O railroad tracks. It was our private reserve with towering Weeping Willows and a small brook flowing through the middle. Also, there was the family junk pile where you would dispose of used jars, cans, and anything the family wanted to discard from the house and barn. I remember the body of a 1916 Ford Model T, including fenders, doors, headlights, etc. My father had stripped the body parts except for the engine and running gear to make it into a buzz saw for sawing wood to burn on cold winter days.

Next to the dump pile was a tall ash tree beside the cold running brook. It was here I envisioned building a shack to play in. In the past, my cousins and I made a stone dam in the summer to back up the water so we could find crayfish and pollywogs. I even found a large 14-inch diameter by 24-inch Lapp high voltage insulator that formed a sluice gate for channeling the water.

In the summer of 1945, my cousin Charlie Longhany and I decided to build the shack as our private clubhouse. I never gave a thought or asked my dad for any supplies or the use of his tools as well. We found four posts eight inches in diameter and six feet long, which would serve as the four corner posts of the shack. Behind the red barn, I found a sheet of corrugated galvanized metal about five feet wide and 8 feet long, which would make a great roof. When it came to the sides of the shack, we found pieces of scrap lumber in the red barn along with a box of nails. We used a handsaw, two hammers, and a hole digger for setting the posts. After putting on the roof and

Billy at the Cold Creek

sides, we discovered the inside was very dark, so we needed a window as well. I found an old oval picture frame with glass in the barn with a picture of an old lady, maybe 30 years or so, and confiscated it for our window. Then there was a need for a door that required two hinges readily found in the barn. The materials and tools had to be carried or placed on the old wooden wheelbarrow, an antique in itself, and transported through the backfield to the shack site.

We were so excited that each day at dinner-time at the Old Brown Table, we would tell the family about our adventure. Dad never questioned our use of materials or tools more likely because he enjoyed seeing our productive efforts put to some use. Well, after two

41

or three days of construction, we stood back and admired our work just as we heard the call for dinner around 5 PM. We were so excited telling all at the Old Brown Table that we had finished our great endeavor, and everyone was invited to see the shack by the cold running brook.

After dinner, we immediately went down to the shack to admire our outstanding achievement. When we reached the site, we were astonished to find the shack was destroyed with the sides lying on the ground, the roof still in place, and the window somehow surviving the tornado-like destruction. Painted on the sideboards in black paint were the words, "Black Hawk Was Here!" We ran as fast as we could to inform Dad and Mom of our horrifying discovery. Dad responded by following us to the site of the destroyed shack and was as puzzled as we were. "Must have been neighborhood kids," he said as he chuckled and walked away. Well, the nearest neighborhood kids were at least a quarter-mile away, and we never met them, but that was more likely the case. They must have heard us hammering away from the B&O railroad tracks, and there was dense foliage between the shack and railroad so they could have easily spied on us.

So, what did we do, but the next day went back to work reconstructing the shack, Black Hawk, or not wondering if someone was watching as we labored away? Black Hawk never returned, fortunately. That shack survived several years and was a fun place in the summer as well as the winter. I found a small cast iron stove in the chicken coup, which my brother Al had used as a workshop for a few years. In the middle of winter, during Christmas vacation, we carted that stove to the shack and installed a smokestack out the rear side facing the cold running brook. I would build a wood fire with kindling wood under a small metal pan taken from the junk pile. I then started the wood fire, and when the pan became very hot, I would pour crude oil into the pan, which then developed a generous flame and heated the shack to a cozy temperature. The only problem is that crude oil would smoke something terrible, and we would return home with blackened faces. When entering the kitchen by the Old Brown table, Mom was perplexed by our coal-mine faces. I did not dare tell her about our new form of energy. Now you are wondering as to where we obtained the crude oil. That is another story, which I will tell later.

Can Mom Climb A Cherry Tree?

On a freezing wintry day in February, Billy went out to play after his Mom helped him with his winter coat, snow-pants, stocking hat, scarf, gloves, and of course, rubber boots. It was a wonder we were able to move in all that gear, but it was winter, and temperatures in upstate New York are usually in the teens.

Billy loved to play outside every day regardless of the temperatures, whether high or low. There was a large white oxheart cherry tree that was always abundant in fruit around July 4th. Just below the tree was a sizable sandbox that was Billy's playpen, many an hour in the summertime.

However, in the winter, Billy liked to climb the tree, not very far in height, but just enough to play an imaginary game. He used to bring up a small iron wheel and play an engineer on the railroad. On this particular winter day, Billy climbed higher than usual, and the view was spectacular in his eyes as he imagined he was that railroad engineer. It was late in the afternoon, and usually, a B&O train would pass through only 500 feet distance at the West lot line, blowing its whistle and spewing out a steady stream of smoke from the coal-burning steam locomotive.

The wind was rather cold that day, and Billy decided it was time to climb down. However, when he looked down, he became frightened since the ground seemed so very far away. What to do? He wasn't sure how he got up so far or what branch to step on to start his way down. What to do, what to do? Well, there was only one thing to do, and that was to call Mom to the rescue.

"Mom, Mom help me. I can't get down. I'm so scared. Please, Mom, help me!" Well, the cries for help went on for some time, and Billy was becoming colder and colder. Now, remember this is winter, and the house is closed uptight, and Mom probably had the radio on. The Old Brown Table heard the cry, but remember it can only hear. After a while, Mom wondered why Billy had not come in for it was at least an hour he had been outside. When she put her head out the back door and called Billy, she heard the frantic cry for help.

Mom put on her winter coat and then saw Billy high up in the Oxheart cherry tree. Without a second thought, she climbed the cherry tree to where Billy was and slowly guided him to a safe landing. That was the first and last time that Mom would ever climb a cherry tree!

Charlie McCarthy Talks

Can a dummy talk? Well, I'm sure you have heard many a dummy talk but in jest, of course. As a young boy growing up in the upstate New York town of Le Roy, I soon became acquainted with Edgar Bergen and Charlie McCarthy when listening to the radio before television came into the home. Every evening after the evening meal at the Old Brown Table, the family would gather in the living room of the old farmhouse to listen to radio programs, which were broadcast on ABC, NBC, and CBS radio networks. This routine was mainly during the winter months when the cold winds and snow would be howling through the old farmhouse walls.

At around seven in the evening, Mom or Dad would turn on the radio to their favorite programs. One of these programs was the Chase and Sanborn Hour, which aired on NBC radio on Sunday nights, 8 to 9 PM, from 1929 to 1948. Edgar Bergen and Charlie McCarthy would weekly appear on this show where Edgar Bergen was a talented ventriloquist, and Charlie McCarthy was his dummy. For several years people listening in thought Charlie McCarthy was a real person until the two appeared in movies and on television in the early 1950s. I remember my Mom saying when she saw Edgar Bergen's lips move, "He is not a good ventriloquist." However, Edgar's real talent was his wit and creating new characters such as Mortimer Snerd and interacting with movie and radio personalities.

As a young 10-year-old boy, Charlie McCarthy not only became a radio star to me but, in fact, entered my life as an actual dummy. At that time, I had an uncle, John Brown, that ran the Valley Hotel on Church Street in Le Roy. Sometimes as a family, we would visit Uncle John and Aunt Mary at their establishment, and Uncle John would bring out his Charlie McCarthy dummy and play ventriloquist, which in no way measured up to Edgar Bergen. It wasn't long before I fell in "love" with Charlie and asked my Dad if I could have a Charlie McCarthy dummy that could talk. So, Dad was not about to buy one for me and instead asked his brother John if he would give me Charlie McCarthy. Uncle John was not the kind of person to give away his valued possessions, but after some persuading, he graciously gave Charlie to me.

I was thrilled to have Charlie and would sit by the radio on Sunday nights, and while I listened to Edgar and Charlie, I would pull the string in the back of Charlie's head, and he would utter the best of jokes and remarks. Here is a conversation with Mae West, a daring pin-up radio star, that Charlie spoke to over the radio waves:

Dickie, Charlie McCarthy & Darlyn

> Charlie: "Not so loud, Mae, not so loud! All my girlfriends are listening."
> Mae: "Oh, yeah! You're all wood and a yard long."
> Charlie: "Yeah."
> Mae: "You weren't so nervous and backward when you came up to see me at my apartment. In fact, you didn't need any encouragement to kiss me."
> Charlie: "Did I do that?"
> Mae: "Why you certainly did. I got marks to prove it. An' splinters, too."

Now that is corny and straightforward humor in today's age, but it certainly was a hit in those innocent years of the '40s and '50s.

Well, in time, Charlie McCarthy aged as we all do, and he became somewhat tattered with paint flaking off his face, and eventually, his speech cord severed, making him mute. Where in time did that dummy doll end up? Only the Old Brown Table knows!

Ref: WikP-Charlie McCarthy

Chemistry Set

As a young child, one of the things I loved to do was to explore the red barn and discover whatever I could find. One day I saw on the ground floor between the joists a cigar box. I found a ladder and brought it down. There were many items in the cigar box covered with a thick layer of dust indicating it had been there for several years. To my surprise, it was a Chemistry Set that was probably given as a Christmas gift to my oldest brother Frank who was 17 years older than I.

After dusting off the test tubes, I found several chemicals and did not know what they were or what you could do with them. There was a burner, which took kerosene, so I brought the set to the Old Brown Table one evening and started to heat some chemicals in a test tube. The result was a terrible smell, which concerned my Dad and Mom. It was then I found out the set was put in the red barn out of sight because they were concerned Frank would mix a poison gas like what happened to a boy Frank's age on the Perry Road. This boy mixed chemicals and created chorine gas, which they say killed him. When Dad and Mom caught the scent of the horrible smell, the chemical set was discarded much to my dismay.

Well, I did not give up because I asked for a Chemistry Set for the following Christmas. Much to my surprise, I received the gift since the store clerk told my parents the sets were very safe today. At the Old Brown Table, I immediately went to work playing with the chemicals. The set included a bottle of liquid called glycerin, which I would heat in a test tube with a cork in it. Upon heating, the pressure would build, and with a loud noise, the cork would blow out, alerting everyone near the table that the mad scientist was again at work.

The next year I received at Christmas a Microscope Set, which opened up a new world for me. At the Old Brown Table, I would view a fly's wing or the fly's head to see the many hundreds of eyes. Looking at the pinhead of a needle to discover, it was rather blunt. Viewing cheese to find things in the cheese that would persuade anyone not to eat it. There was no end to discovery, and another world was opened up to my insatiable curiosity. The Old Brown Table was satisfied as well since I could no longer blow a hole in the kitchen ceiling or spill some terrible chemicals to eat the table finish.

Dad Fell Off the Roof

The Fall was always the time to make preparations for the harsh upstate New York winter. Takedown screens, put up storm windows, and move the porch furniture to the barn was the usual routine right after the grape harvest was completed. Cleaning out the furnace chimney was an unusual task Dad would perform. I mention it was notable because of the method of cleaning. Dad would take some spent D-size flashlight batteries, break them open to expose the carbon, light them with a torch and drop them down the chimney to burn out the creosote.

On October 9, 1941 he came home from work for lunch and decided to clean out the chimney. He was most likely in a hurry since he had to be back to work after his lunch break. Dad used an extension ladder to reach the roof and carried up an old wooden stepladder to prop against the chimney and the roof. It had rained the night before, so the roof was slippery. When he got on the stepladder, it slipped, and he fell to the ground 30 feet below, just missing the top of the concrete rainwater tank by a few inches. The stepladder came down immediately after him striking him in the back. Mom heard the fall and his crying out for help. She had to run next door to Mrs. Meehan since they did not have a telephone at that time. Dr. Welsh arrived from Le Roy around 15 minutes later and the ambulance 20 minutes after the doctor. Dad was taken to St. Jerome Hospital in Batavia and was listed in critical condition. Dad had a few cracked ribs but fortunately, did not have any significant fractures though he developed blood clots in his leg, which if reached his heart, could kill him.

In May of 1941, his son Frank was called to serve in the Army and was currently in training at Ft. Dix, NJ. Mom did not want to alarm Frank so far from home, so she only wrote on October 10th that he had a fall. Since dad's condition was severe, she wrote three letters in the next two days but leaving out considerable detail. Frank wrote back, "I was surprised to hear Dad is in the hospital. I had a feeling something was wrong. Tell him to take care of himself and do just as the doctor says. He shouldn't get up until the doctors say that he can." Frank sensing Mom was not telling all about Dad's condition, tried to get an emergency pass. At this time, Frank was told by the First Sergeant that all men who failed to make a qualifying score with the rifle need not expect furloughs or passes. You can be sure that was reason enough to improve his rifle score.

On October 18th, Frank got a three-day pass to go home because of the family emergency. He left Ft. Dix, NJ, at 1 pm, caught a bus from Trenton to Newark and from Newark to Batavia, arriving home at 5 am Sunday. He surprised everyone and found Dad to be very sick. On Sunday, after Frank arrived, Dad went home against the doctor's orders. He was taken home by ambulance and brought in the house by the Old Brown Table to the bedroom in front of the house. After being home for only 10 hours, Frank left at 3 pm on a train for New York City and connected to Ft. Dix arriving at 4:30 am. Dad would be laid up in bed at home for several weeks due to the blood clot in his leg. At this very time, his daughter Eleanor had already set a date for her wedding to Manny Costa for October 25th. Unfortunately, Dad could not walk her down the aisle but had to remain in bed at home.

The following weeks were challenging for the family since there was no insurance to cover lost wages or insurance for the hospital and doctor expenses. The Old Brown Table heard many discussions on how the bills would be paid for the next several months. Frank volunteered to contribute a few dollars from his low rank of Private. Al and Eleanor were working and would help out as well. It was a wonderful time for the family to support each other in this challenging period, as witnessed by the Old Brown Table.

Ellis Chocolate Easter Egg

In late 1940 my sister Eleanor, starting dating Dominic (Manny) Costa, who resided with his parents in Lime Rock. Manny was a handsome, tall thin man who possessed a sharp 1936 black Plymouth Coupe for taking Eleanor on dates.

Around Easter, in 1941, Manny surprised Eleanor with a giant chocolate Easter egg that he purchased from E. G. Ellis in Le Roy. I remember I was only six years old at the time when Manny brought the giant chocolate egg into the kitchen and sat it on the Old Brown Table. I was astonished at the size of the egg decorated with a colored frosting design and displaying many candies around the outside of the egg. I never saw so much chocolate in my life, and I couldn't wait to be offered some. Well, Eleanor could not do that right away, for, after all, it was a gift from her beau.

E. G. Ellis made the egg, and it was in his front display window at his Main Street candy store near the Le Roy Theatre. Ellis was an excellent candy maker, and our family often bought chocolate candy and ice cream at his store. He had a soda fountain, and I fondly remember chocolate sodas and milkshakes. The store was furnished with a dark finish counter and stools, display cases loaded with candy, and several dark varnished booths for eating ice cream treats.

The Le Roy Gazette dated January 5, 1939, shows an ad for Ellis, which listed Chocolate Clusters and Peanut candy at 25 cents/lb. Now 25 cents/lb. appears cheap but adjusted by inflation to 2020, it would be $4.39/lb. Can you imagine what that chocolate egg cost, probably at least $20? Manny was indeed serious on Eleanor, and shortly after that, the date for marriage was set for October 1941.

The large Chocolate Easter Egg did not last long once a knife cut off a piece of that delicious chocolate. Everyone in the household had their fill of milk chocolate except, of course, the Old Brown Table.

LRGN: 1-5-1939

Front Yard Antics

Now well into my senior years, it is always amusing to tell my grandchildren stories about my youth, some stories with life lessons, and some just plain funny. When recalling these tales, I can't help but wonder how much the Old Brown Table heard these tales when I was a child.

The front yard of our country farmhouse was very spacious boarded in front by Rt. 19, Warsaw Road, and two neatly trimmed hedges on the north and south side of the old farmhouse. Now the front lawn needed mowing usually once a week during the late spring and early summer, and that, of course, was my job. In between, however, this space became a frequent playground and an excellent spot to view the fast traffic on the state highway.

One activity I will always remember is watching for the trucks taking harvested vines with pea pods to the canning factory in Le Roy. These trucks were so overloaded they would often lose a bunch of vines with their clinging pea pods. As soon as a truck would lose a bunch of vines, I would rush into the roadway, seize the vines and rush back to the lawn where I would have a feast breaking open the pods and using my front teeth to swipe those delicious sweet peas into my mouth. If you have never experienced this in your lifetime, you indeed have missed something.

Have you ever discovered a new toy by chance and did not realize the potential for the future? One day I took from my Mom's utensils a tin pie pan and wondered if I could make it sail. I went to the front yard, and to my amazement, I could throw the pie pan, and it would sail smoothly through the air for a reasonable distance. Again, and again I would throw the pie pan and, with a spin from the wrist, could increase the distance and provide more stability. I did not realize at the time that I had made a homemade frisbee before they were ever on the market.

In 1937 Walter F. Morrison had fun tossing a popcorn can lid after a Thanksgiving Day dinner, and he soon discovered a market for a flying disc when he offered 25 cents for a cake pan that you could toss back and forth on a beach near Los Angeles, CA. After World

War II, Morrison sketched a design for an aerodynamically improved flying disc that he called the WhirloWay after the famous racehorse. He and business partner Warren Franscioni began producing the first plastic discs by 1948 after experimentation with several prototypes. They renamed it the Flyin-Saucer until the two of them once overheard someone saying that the pair were using wires to make the discs hover so they developed a sales pitch, "The Flyin-Saucer is free, but the invisible wire is $1." Morrison designed a new model in 1955 called the Pluto Platter, the archetype of all modern flying discs. He sold the rights to Wham-O on January 23, 1957, and the rest is Frisbee's history. Wow, did I miss out on that invention, and yes, Mom wanted her pie pan back!

There were a few incidents that were rather daring for front yard antics when my cousin Chuckie Gallagher, two years older than I, spent two weeks at our home during our summer vacation. One day we went into the woods and, with our sharp pocket knives, cut two small tree limbs which we fashioned into a bow. Then we cut some pencil size limbs from bushes and made some arrows. We practiced shooting the arrows at objects like Blackie, the cat, and Pal, my favorite dog, both of whom did not appreciate our fun. None of these targets enjoyed our bow and arrow practice, so we decided we needed a more sophisticated target. Our fateful choice was moving cars and trucks on Rt. 19, which we soon were to regret. It was great fun, and a challenge since the vehicles were traveling at an incredible speed, and we had trouble making our mark. Then a

Chuckie & Billy

car approached moving at a slower speed, and from our concealed perch behind a large maple tree, we took aim and let the arrows sail forth. To our amazement, we both hit the back fender of the car. To an even greater surprise, the car slowed, stopped, and turned around at the Cole Road intersection and Rt. 19. On its return, we could see an agitated older couple in the car with the woman pointing her finger at us. In terror, we made a run for the woodshed behind the house, dropping our weapons on the way. We heard the car in the driveway, and a man and woman very agitated, complaining to my Mom. Then to our horror, my Dad arrived home from work at the worst possible time and heard the couple spew out these terrible accusations that two young boys were trying to kill them with bows and arrows.

Now we were in between a rock and a hard place, as you would say. If we leave the woodshed, we would have to face these angry accusers, and if we stayed, we would miss suppertime. Being growing hungry boys, we choose not to ignore the most important meal of the day regardless of the consequences. Well, the Old Brown Table heard a scolding at the dinner table that afternoon. We both took it well and vowed we would never shoot at cars or anything that could cause harm even with bows and arrows that could barely kill a fly.

One day I picked up a box that had fallen off a truck, thinking I would find something valuable inside. It was empty, of course, but it gave me the idea to plant a box along the side of the road, fill it with rocks and see how many people would try to pick it up. After sitting on the front porch for an endless hour, not a single vehicle stopped so that promptly ended that psychological experiment.

As a young boy, I had several chores to perform, including feeding the chickens, collecting eggs, trimming the two hedges that bordered the front yard, and of course, mowing the lawn. Mowing was not so bad, but I hated cutting those hedges. It took a lot of care to make sure they were cut even. The lawn could be cut in nice straight rows, that is, until I presented the hand-pushed lawnmower to my second cousin, Chuckie Gallagher, when visiting during the summer vacation. Just as I thought I might have some slave labor to help me, Chuckie pushed the mower in crooked circles over the lawn. That action prompted a fast response from me loudly, informing Chuckie he was crazy to cut a lawn in that fashion. My comment led to a fight with neither of us getting hurt except our pride and feelings. The Old Brown Table heard a complaint that evening, but it did not solicit affirmation but instead a lot of laughs.

I enjoyed making paper and balsa wood airplanes as a teenager and, of course, flying them out of my upstairs bedroom window onto the front yard. The balsa wood airplanes were crudely made from a drawing in a magazine. Their flight path was not very remarkable, of course, sometimes crashing in an uncontrolled dive to the ground. My parents then bought me a Piper Cub balsa plane kit, which I enthusiastically put together after several hours of work. The small model plane with a wingspan of just 14 inches had a windup rubber band driven propeller to permit the aircraft to fly for several seconds. I debated as to whether I should try a flight from the bedroom window since a crash could demolish my hours of fabrication. I soon concluded that what good is a model airplane if you don't attempt flight. After all, that is what planes do! So, with much trepidation, I opened my bedroom window, wound the propeller as tightly as I could, held it out the window, and let go with a slight forward throw. Well, the plane headed straight for Rt. 19, and all I could see was it being run over by a big truck. Fortunately, it did not have sufficient power to reach the road but came down hard in the freshly cut lawn, doing some damage to one wing. That was the end of the flight for my precious plane. From now on, it would take a proud position on my desk for all to see and admire.

Ref: WikP-Frisbee

High School Renovation Hazards

On June 16, 1949, the Le Roy Community voted on the establishment of a Central School District, which included the proposed centralization of School Districts Nos. 1,3,5,6,7,8,10 and 11 of the town of Le Roy and District No. 1 of Stafford. If approved, the existing property of Le Roy public Schools, with alterations in the high school building and the erection of a new auditorium, gymnasium, cafeteria, and kitchen, would become the new high school. A lay committee presented a study during the past year that showed the present facilities did not afford room for additional pupils or enable a curriculum that measured up to communities comparable to Le Roy. The estimated cost for a tentative plan by the State Education Department was $1,218,000, of which the state would provide 38% or $462,000. Many local taxpayers were concerned about the cost and the resultant increase in taxes over the next several years. However, the voters responded with approval of 696 versus 50 against the measure.

On September 23, 1949, the voters approved a $1,196,040 ($13,000,000 in 2020 dollars) bond issue by a vote of 785 to 129. This approval paved the way for the erection of a new auditorium and gymnasium and alterations of the present school buildings. Construction then commenced from 1950 through 1951. The new auditorium and gymnasium would be named Memorial Auditorium for those that gave their lives in WWII, which pleased the voters since there was some opposition to these new facilities. At the Old Brown Table, this subject was discussed to some length with general approval since the present gym was so small, and the ceiling height was so limited that when a basketball player shot baskets, they would often hit the ceiling supports.

On Wednesday, May 1, 1951, a beautiful sunny warm day, the cornerstone was laid at the Memorial Auditorium building. There were 500 students seated on the lawn with parents and teachers grouped around them. It was an impressive sight with the colorful red and black uniforms of the school band sitting near the building, the flags flanking the speaker's platform, and Old Glory floating in the breeze from the school staff at Trigon Park. The program opened with a processional, "The Oatkan March," written by William Lane, instructor of music at the school who directed the band. School Superintendent Matthew W. Gaffney presided over the program and presented local dignitaries, some of which gave short speeches covering different phases of the building program.

Memorial Auditorium

During the coming months in 1950 and 1951, there was considerable construction activity on the school grounds, which the students could well testify to since school was in process during the construction. A corner or section of the building would be closed off where the construction workers would jackhammer concrete, hammer, drill, and perform other construction activities that sometimes would override the voice of the teacher. Then one day, the unpredictable finally happened. We were in Mr. Jim Perrone's math class with the loud noise of jackhammering in the classroom directly above us. Suddenly the jackhammer broke through the ceiling with a cloud of dust resulting in a large chunk of concrete falling into our room, hitting the pencil sharpener, and tearing it off the wall. As our eyes widened with fear, Mr. Perrone shouted over the jackhammer noise with a calm, clear voice, "Class Leave Now." We exited immediately with calmness and laughing with glee that our class would now be terminated. Well, not the case since the Principle, Dr. Donald Horr, found an empty classroom in 15 minutes, so the teaching resumed. The Old Brown Table heard a good story that night at dinner with concern expressed by my mom. I, being a teenager, thought this was indeed a great adventure.

LRGN: 6-9-1949; 6-23-1949; 9-29-1949.

Horrific Grind

The Old Brown Table served many functions, including the preparation of many foods such as preparing fresh peaches, tomatoes pears, or corn for canning. Sometimes it would be cracking black walnuts and then the difficult picking of the small nuts in the little shell crevices. Since the table was in the center of the kitchen and all indoor/outdoor traffic passed through it to the house interior, it was commonplace for conversation.

One day in late summer, my Dad said he had a chore for me concerning grinding up a vegetable. The grinder was a hand-cranked cast metal type that was used for grinding many different types of meat, fruits, and vegetables. On this occasion, Dad brought in what looked like giant white carrots. He told me to wash them off thoroughly and scrape them gently to remove some of the skin. Then

I was to place them in the grinder with a coarse grind setting. The grinder, set on the edge of the Old Brown Table, was attached with the tightening of a thumb-screw. Those thumb screw marks are on the Old Brown Table to this day. Then a pan was placed on the floor to catch the juice or spillage. Also, a pan under the grinder outlet to catch the ground material.

So, following my Dad's instruction, I loaded up the mouth of the grinder and started turning the crank, thinking this was going to be a quick chore. A whitish juice started dripping onto the floor pan, and white material came out of the grinder. All seemed to be going well, although the smell was quite strong, when all of a sudden, I could not breathe. My nose and eyes started to burn terribly, and then almost instantly, my throat closed up, and I could not get my breath. My eyes burning out of my head, I made a rush for the back door, and once outside, I gasped for breath. It took a few minutes before my watering eyes started to clear and I could breathe normally again, but still with a burning sensation in my nose.

What was this horrible substance? My Mom and Dad started to laugh when they told me I was grinding horseradish, which not only exhibited a significant effect on the taste buds and throat cavity, but the juice had a double whammy effect on the eyes, throat, and lungs. They told me to try again but with a fan on the grinder to whisk away the harsh fumes.

Well, I finished the job with much tribulation as witnessed by the Old Brown Table and always vowed to respect the wild in-ground vegetable called Horse Radish. I'm convinced horses did not like it either!

Jack, Do You Believe in God?

Dad worked most of his life as a cast-iron molder at the Le Roy Plow Works. They made various farm implements from cast iron, such as plows for tilling farm fields. It was a dirty job, dusty and strenuous, and extremely hot in the summer. In 1945 the doctor informed him that he had spots on his lungs most likely from ingesting sand dust over several years. He was told that he had to find another job with a clean working environment. He soon found a job working for Ernest and Edith Woodward at their large estate on East Main Street in Le Roy called Popular Lane Farm. They wanted a gardener to restore their flowerbeds, which had been overgrown with weeds and bushes for several years. Also, he was to re-open their private greenhouse to provide fresh vegetables and flowers year-round. The flower gardens were overgrown with brush and weeds, and it was taking a great deal of effort over a few months just to clear it out and develop the soil. The greenhouse also needed repair, and the hot water heating system was brought back in operation.

Woodward Flower Gardens

One day in the summer of 1947, my Dad came home from work at his usual time around 5 PM, and when he settled down to dinner at the Old Brown Table, he related a conversation he had with his employer Ernest Woodward. It was a sweltering summer day, and Dad was pulling out weeds from the outdoor flower gardens. Without his knowledge Ernest Woodward was standing directly behind him and with a profound voice said, "Jack, do you believe in God?" Dad was so startled that he did not perceive the question at first and looked up at Mr. Woodward with perspiration running down his face. Dad then replied, "Yes, I do and have all of my life." I wish I knew the conversation that question started, and if Mr. Woodward had any doubts about God and eternity, it was answered in the discussion that followed. This vital discussion could have included the following message.

Everyone in their respective lifetime will face the question, where will I go when I die?" Ernest was experiencing health problems in his senior years and most likely was facing this question. If we believe in God, will that secure us a place in heaven for eternity? A challenging question that has an answer but not the one most of us expect.

First of all, we must recognize our sin: Romans 3:23, "for all have sinned and fall short of the Glory of God."

So, then this begs the question, where will we go? Is it the eternal state of heaven or hell? The answer for the road to heaven is: Romans 6:23, "For the wages of sin is death, but the free gift of God is eternal life in Christ Jesus our Lord."

But how is this accomplished if we are such sinners all of our life? The answer is Romans 5:8, "but God shows his love for us in that while we were still sinners, Christ died for us."

So, God, who loves you despite your sins, sent Jesus Christ to take the punishment for your sins on Himself. Therefore, as best stated in Romans 10:9-10, 13: "that, if you confess with your mouth that Jesus is Lord and believe in your heart that God raised him from the dead, you will be saved. For with the heart, one believes and is justified, and with the mouth, one confesses and is saved. For everyone who calls on the name of the Lord will be saved."

At this time, it is believed Mr. Woodward knew he had a heart condition at the age of 65 and realized he was in a critical stage of his life when he was facing the prospect of death. That fall, he finalized his last will on November 6, 1947. It should be noted that Ernest Woodward was a religious man, attended St. Mark's Episcopal Church in Le Roy and served as vestryman.

I remember him well since I met him with my Dad several times at the estate, either at the greenhouse and gardens or at the mansion. Since I started at Le Roy High School in January 1948 and there was no bus transportation, my Dad would take me to school in the morning on his way to work. After school, I would walk to the Woodward estate on East Main Street and meet my Dad at the greenhouse or in the flower gardens. Sometimes Ernest Woodward would be there talking to Dad, and sometimes we would meet him at the mansion when Dad needed to inform him about a matter. For a young 11-year-old boy, he impressed me as a very kind distinguished man and, of course, ancient from my young perspective. Mr. Woodward liked to kid around and questioned me about school and what I wanted to be when I grew up. I did not realize at the time what a talented gentleman this person was and what outstanding accomplishments he had achieved in his life.

Ernest Woodward was born on October 20, 1882, the eldest son of Orator F. and Cora Talmadge Woodward and attended Le Roy Academy and Preparatory schools. He went to work for his father, who was then laying the foundation for the Jell-O Company, known then as the Genesee Pure Foods Company, and operated the manufacture of proprietary medicine under the name of O. F. Woodward. Ernest married Edith Hartwell, a schoolteacher, on December 31, 1903. When his father's health failed in 1905, he took over the business, and on his father's death in January 1906, he became president. Under his management, the company grew fast, and Jell-O became its principal product. In December 1925, the Jell-O Company and the Postum Cereal Company were merged with the stock valued at $64,410,000 ($945,800,000 in 2020 dollars). At the close of the 1920s, just before the stock market crash, the company had around 600 employees, and by 1948 there were four other Jell-O plants in the US, a fifth in Mexico and a sixth in Canada. They were then part of the $171,000,000 General Foods Corp.

Ernest Woodward

Ernest Woodward was a community and national leader with a long list of accomplishments. On his retirement from business operations at a young age of 43, he had more time to devote to his other interests. In 1921 he aided in the organization for the Stafford Country Club, served three years as the first president, and gave liberally to the club when a $60000 bond issue was retired in 1922. In 1927 he acquired a winter home in Camden, SC, and revived the Springdale Steeplechase Course and donated the Carolina Cup. The Carolinas Cup Races were run every spring from 1930 to 1942 when they were discontinued because of the war.

He joined the Genesee Valley Hunt Club at Geneseo and rode horses for several seasons. Ernest was devoted to rod and gun sports and purchased several hundred acres in the North Woods northeast of

Le Roy and established a game preserve. In other endeavors, he was director of the Security Trust Company of Rochester for several years and director of the Bank of Le Roy from 1932 to 1935. It was rumored that he saved the Bank of Le Roy after the stock market crash on October 29, 1929, by backing it with his security, thus keeping the Le Roy residents from losing all of their savings. The bank in Bergen and thousands of banks throughout the nation were not so lucky, and many lost all they had in their accounts. The Federal Deposit Insurance Corporation did not exist until the 1933 Banking Act, insuring deposits at banks and savings institutions.

Even in World War I, when Ernest was 35 years old, he was given charge of Red Cross shipping at Norfolk, VA. He donated a Ford Model T ambulance to be driven by Malcolm Olson of Le Roy, who was serving with the Red Cross in Italy. While the ambulance was in transport to Italy, the vessel on which it was being carried was torpedoed. The ambulance was lost, but Mr. Woodward promptly secured another vehicle.

Woodward was a lifelong Republican and contributed to the national state and local campaign funds. He was a delegate to the 1912 convention in St. Louis at the age of 30 that nominated Charles H. Hughes and was a presidential elector in support of Hughes.

The above is an approximate mention of the many generous gifts Ernest Woodward provided to the citizens of Le Roy and the surrounding community. The best gift of all was steady employment at the Jell-O factory in Le Roy, where my brother Frank, Alfred, and sister Eleanor worked for several years. Frank worked as a tinsmith at the plant for four years until he was drafted into the Army in May 1941. A plaque at the Jell-O Gallery today honors his service as one of two employees who gave their lives in WWII. It wasn't until 1964 that the General Foods Company decided to close the Le Roy plant and move its operation to Dover, DE., which ended an era of the Jell-O production in the Le Roy community.

On April 22, 1948, Dad came home from work and sadly announced at the Old Brown Table that Ernest Woodward had passed away that day. Dad expressed how fortunate we were to know this man with a recollection of his magnificent contributions to the Le Roy community over the past several years.

LRGN: 6-20-1917; 9-12-1928; 1-29-1930; 4-22-1948.

James P. Tountas
Lunch, Candy, Ice Cream & More

There were two stores in Le Roy where you could buy handcrafted candy and ice cream. One was the Ellis Ice Cream Shop close to the Le Roy Theatre and the Tountas Coffee Shoppe west up Main Street about five storefronts. The name "coffee shop" did not represent the many products he offered for sale. During the Great Depression in 1933, you could rent a Jig Saw puzzle instead of buying it. At times he sold greeting cards and baked goods like homemade bread, pecan rolls, or a braided coffee ring, and in 1950 you could lunch on sandwiches and salads.

I was more familiar with the Tountas shop since my sister Eleanor worked there in the mid-1940s when I was in grade school. Saturday was always a special day of the week since my parents would take me to town to attend the Le Roy Theatre afternoon matinee for a ticket price of 15 cents. After the show, I would walk up the street to the Tountas Coffee Shoppe and have my sister make me a chocolate soda for 15 cents. I preferred chocolate milkshakes, but they cost about 10 cents more, and I was not given enough to make that purchase. There were also the Le Roy Cut Rate Drugs on Main Street, where the kids would go after the matinee, but my sister did not work there, so Tountas was the choice.

James P. Tountas

James P. Tountas advertised on July 3, 1941, Gazette News that to "Keep Cool" come to his store that was "Completely Air-Conditioned for your comfort and health." Home air-conditioning was not around in the 1940s and did not make it into homes until 20 years later. On a hot summer day in Le Roy, it was delightful to enjoy the cool Le Roy Theatre or one of the stores that had the foresight to have air conditioning installed. Tountas advertised, "You are invited to come at any time and relax and cool off. Enjoy a soda or luncheon at our fountain or booths."

Tountas displayed many varieties of handmade candy in the long case to the right as you entered the store. The soda fountain with round stools anchored to the floor was on the left. The store was opened on Saturday, May 24, 1930, when Tountas moved from the O'Shea block next to the Medical Hall, his original store that he owned. The new store housed a bakery, soda fountain, lunch counter, booths with total seating for 100 people.

Although the candy was the best in town, our favorite ice cream was in the form of an "ice cream pie." Dad would buy one and bring it home, usually on Saturday night, and Mom would cut it on the Old Brown Table. I believed this was the best ice cream in the whole world. During World War Two, Dad would buy a variety of candy to mail to his son Frank who was in service at Camp Gordan, Augusta, Georgia. Frank would write back on how the candy would go in one setting with all of the men in his barracks partaking.

Tountas came to the USA when he was 14 years old and worked hard to establish his business over the years. He was very civic-minded, and every year in the 40s and 50s, he would host a dinner for the Le Roy Senior class at the Coffee Shoppe on the second floor. He also would give each senior a gold pin designed especially for that year. My class of 1953 was no exception when he provided dinner to all 77 graduates with the 53-gold pin. His generosity was appreciated for many years, even after a fire severely damaged his business on March 4, 1945. He rebuilt and continued to operate his business at 52 Main Street until retiring on July 1, 1961.

The Old Brown Table will indeed remember James P. Tountas for his generosity to the Le Roy community and the delectable ice cream, candy, and of course, the "Ice Cream Pie."

LRGN: 5-31-1930; 6-2-1949; 6-15-1950; 5-24-1951; 6-7-1951.

Le Roy Theatre and Adorable Cheeta

Billy usually attended movies on Saturday afternoon at the Le Roy Theatre. He would view such pictures as "The Paleface" starring Bob Hope and Jane Russell and "Jungle Goddess" with George Reeves showing on January 21-22, 1949. Then, of course, were the cowboy westerns like Roy Rogers and Hopalong Cassidy and who could forget "Bud Abbott and Lou Costello Meet the Killer Boris Karloff," showing on September 11-13, 1949. Billy never forgot the space thriller, "The Thing, From Another World," showing on May 22-24, 1951. It was so real in your mind that when you left the theatre, it would keep playing in your head like it was as natural as life. Of course, this occurred at the time when flying saucers were showing up all over the planet with little green men.

Le Roy Theatre LRHS

Billy loved the movies and, at the keen age of seven, viewed several of the Tarzan features with Johnny Weissmuller as Tarzan, Maureen O'Sullivan as Jane and the sweet, charming monkey named Cheeta. Now Billy's pick for the most adored creature was not Jane but Cheeta. He fell in love with Cheeta and begged his Mom and Dad for a monkey household pet. The answer to this logical request was a resounding NO, but shortly after that, Billy had a black cat named Blackie and then came his most adored pet, a dog named Pal. All of this did not measure up to Cheeta!

When Billy became a teenager, a new challenge arose for the Le Roy Theatre. A few teenagers attending the theatre routinely were loud and disruptive, much to the concern of adults and some children as well. The disruptive behavior led to a letter directed to the editor of the Le Roy Gazette News, dated January 20, 1949, which on the front page read, "Student Council Deplores Behavior." It stated, "We, the youth of Le Roy, would like to offer our sincerest apologies for the bad conduct of these disrespectful people. Steps should be taken for the disapproval of this, a rather deplorable condition of which we are heartily ashamed. There are some seven hundred boys and girls in Le Roy, and most of them do attend the movies. Of this number, perhaps a dozen or so are the ones who disturb the theatre audience. We just wish to assure you that we are ashamed of the behavior of those people, and measures will be taken to improve the situation and guarantee your movie visits to be peaceful." Signed sincerely, James Arrington President of Student Council, and Joyce Mooney, Vice President.

I wonder what Cheeta and The Old Brown Table would have thought?

LRGN: 1-20-1949.

Limburger Stink

Now I like just about all kinds of cheese except one in particular called Limburger. I was introduced to this cheese when growing up as a young child by my parents visiting Uncle Bob and Aunt Katie. Aunt Katie was crippled her entire life and wore a high block shoe on the shortened side and had to use a crutch and a cane to walk. I always marveled at how well she would get around her kitchen in the small one and half story house in Mumford, NY, just to the rear of the Post Office. My parents and I would usually visit on Friday night, and they would engage in family conversation in which I had no interest. However, at 10 PM, Aunt Katie would enter her small kitchen with a large round table and start preparing snacks. Now Bob and Katie's home was very primitive compared to our old farmhouse since it did not have running water or a standard bathroom. You would work a small hand pump over the kitchen sink, which pulled water from a well just outside the house. The bathroom was an outside toilet in the garage, which I never wanted to use for obvious reasons.

Now, Aunt Katie's late evening spread was something to behold. She would have saltine crackers, braunschweiger sausage (liverwurst), pig hocks, pepperoni, salami, jams, jellies, Velveeta cheese, mozzarella cheese, and the famous stinky Limburger cheese. Now I relished all of these food morsels except the pig hocks, which were taken from a large glass jar and the Limburger cheese from a small tub. As soon as the lid from the Limburger tub was removed, this pungent stink filled the small kitchen and then increased in intensity as my Dad and Uncle Bob spread this soft cheese on crackers or even worse on a sandwich. Then came the pig hocks, which was cholesterol on steroids. When I was offered a hock, I politely turned it down since I could only detect a small sliver of pork wrapped in layers of soft fat. I concentrated on the yellow soft Velveeta cheese, salami, and liverwurst, followed by a giant homemade cookie and glass of milk.

What puzzled me was upon leaving around 11 PM and traveling seven miles back home in the 1936 Chevy sedan my father upon entering our kitchen at the Old Brown Table would exclaim, "Why do they always have Velveeta cheese. Limburger has it beat by a mile." He was right on the money because you could smell Limburger for at least a mile!

Main Street Fire

On Sunday, March 4, 1945, our family left for church at 7:15 am for the 7:30 mass at St. Joseph's Church on Lake Street. It was a cold March morning with the temperature just above freezing and a cold wind of 15 MPH out of the Northwest. Just after our 36 Chevy left the homestead, we noticed a large cloud of black smoke over the center of Le Roy, indicating a large fire was in progress. As we traveled down Clay Street heading north, we could hear sirens in the distance as we chattered about the possible location of the fire. We crossed Main Street by the Fire Station and Town Hall and, to our horror, saw a massive fire on the north side of Main Street west of the Le Roy Theatre. We continued on and attended the 7:30 am Mass, where the priest asked us to pray for the firefighters to control the massive fire. It was hard to concentrate on the church service hearing the sirens in the distance and not knowing what was occurring at the fire.

After church, we parked on Clay Street and walked up to the fire, which was still underway with several fire companies present. Firefighters had several hoses trained on the roaring blaze being fanned by the northwest wind. The tall second and third story windows were broken out, bellowing fire and smoke while firefighters desperately tried to get the fire under control. We only stayed for about 15 minutes while the cold wind cut through our go to church clothing, and Dad gave the command to return home. Later in the day at the Old Brown Table, Dad told us that someone was missing and presumed lost in the fire. Later in the week, the Thursday edition of the Le Roy Gazette News reported the grim details of this disastrous fire.

This was the worst fire for the Main Street business section since the winter of 1902 when the same block was utterly gutted. It was believed the fire started at 4:45 am on Sunday and burned for four hours until it was finally brought under control. One man was dead, and two firemen were slightly injured with a total estimated cost of $250,000 ($3,600,000 in 2020 dollars). The Le Roy fire company was assisted by Batavia, Brockport, Caledonia, and Warsaw. There were several explosions in what was called the Lampson block, and flames spread quickly throughout the three-story structure. After the fire, only a skeleton of the front wall on Main Street was standing.

Main Street Fire

According to the Le Roy Gazette News, Mario Agnello of Seneca Falls was visiting his grandparents, Mr. and Mrs. Charles Mogavero, of 11 Bacon Street, opposite the fire when they heard the screams of Mrs. Alex from the burning building.

Securing two ladders at the rear of the Tountas Coffee Shoppe, they succeeded in bringing Mrs. Alex to safety just before an explosion brought down part of the rear wall. The rescuers did not see Mr. Alex, but according to his wife, he left her at the window and turned back to make sure all tenants had been awakened. The Connors, who were tenants, told firefighters that when they reached the front fire escape, Mr. Alex arrived and then turned back into the building to return to his wife. Later it was presumed he was overcome by smoke or felled by the explosion. Other tenants in the Panepento and Jones building escaped down the front fire escape and were aided by the firemen. My Dad told us at the Old Brown Table on Wednesday evening that Mr. Alex's body was recovered from under the stairway that led from the ground floor to the second and third stories. I was distraught at the thought of someone dying in a fire in their attempt to escape while trying to help others. Dad said he was a restaurant proprietor in Le Roy and a very respected gentleman.

Several business occupants that were temporally relocated were the Danahy-Faxon Grocery, Le Roy Liquor Store, Dr. J. Edward Murray Dental Office, Selective Service Office, O. L. F. Co-Operative, Sidney D. O'Shea Office, and the Rotary Club. J. P. Tountas would continue to operate from his storefront on a limited basis until building repairs were made. In summary, this was a disastrous fire for Le Roy due to the large property loss, and it would take a few years to build a new structure to establish new offices and storefronts.

LRGN: 3-8-1945

Missing Only Two Months

On Friday, April 16, 1948, my dad came home from work at his usual time around 5 pm and had some shocking news. At the time, he was employed by Ernest and Edith Woodward at their large estate on East Main Street called Popular Lane Farm. He started working for Ernest Woodward in mid-1945 when they were interested in starting up the greenhouse and restoring the flower gardens after being dormant for several years.

In April 1948, Mr. Woodward planned to visit his son Talmadge and family in Santa Fe, NM. Talmadge, his wife, and family had moved there in April 1947, and it was rumored that they were having marital problems. Ernest hired a private plane to make the trip, but since he had a heart condition, the doctor advised him to take the railroad. The high altitude in an aircraft could place a strain on his heart due to the lower oxygen content, and it would present a risk. However, he disregarded the doctor's orders and took the private plane. He made the trip okay, but while in Santa Fe, he suffered a heart attack, which was fatal.

A week later, in the Le Roy Gazette News, there were details on Ernest Woodward's last will, part of which read, "To each person in his employ in and around his residence and grounds for three years continuing only just before his death he bequeathed $5000." Dad quickly calculated his time of continuous employment, and it amounted to two years and ten months, which, of course, lacked two months for the specified period of three years. Weeks later, he was informed that he would not receive the amount of $5000 or any amount from the will. Not getting any inheritance was indeed a disappointment for Dad and Mom since if you allow for inflation to 2020, the amount is equivalent to $32130. At that time, Dad was only earning about $3120 per year or about $1.50 per hour. The Old Brown Table heard many a conversation as to whether Mrs. Edith Woodward would make an exception so that Dad would be compensated in another way. As time would tell, that would not come to pass. Dad, in time, accepted the unusual circumstance and remained faithful to Mrs. Edith Woodward for the next several years.

Ernest & Edith Woodward Mansion

However, as the years passed, the servants at the Popular Lane Farm mansion were becoming concerned about Edith Woodward's health. She lost a considerable amount of weight after her husband Ernest died, and she lived on a very meager amount of food. Dad said she always wanted fresh lettuce from the greenhouse, but her personal maid told dad that she ate like a bird. She started to care less about the mansion, and it showed in the lace curtains that now showed wear. One day during the winter, Dad was called to the office by Miss. Mcleod, Edith's personal secretary, and questioned about the amount of fuel oil the greenhouse was using. She thought the monthly bill was high compared to the garage. Rather strange coming from a multimillionaire and among other things, it was an irritation to Dad.

In October 1955, Edith was admitted to Strong Memorial Hospital in Rochester, and the staff was now very concerned about her health. In just a few days, she passed away on Saturday, October 8, 1955, at 7:45 AM at the age of 77. The last will of Edith Hartwell Woodward was presented for probate in Surrogate's Court in Batavia on Monday, October 24th, which disposed of an estate estimated at $12,000,000 ($115,574,000 in 2020 dollars). When Dad read the paper, he was surprised by the gifts to the Woodward staff. The will read, "Employees of Mrs. Woodward are remembered in the will. She directed that all who are employed full time and for one year immediately before her death shall be paid $300 each and an additional $500 for each additional full year." Since dad had been employed for nine years, his gift would be $4800 ($46230 in 2020 dollars), a very generous gift indeed. At the Old Brown Table, Dad noted how Edith wanted to recognize employees with only one year or more of employment as compared to her husband's will where a minimum of three years was required. Edith, of course, knew about my Dad not receiving any gift by missing two months when her husband died and did not want to see that happen again to any of her

Edith Woodward

employees. A true testimony to the kind and compassionate person she exhibited throughout her life.

When I was with my Dad, I met her several times, either at the mansion or in her gardens. She always greeted me with a smile and asked how I was doing in school. I did not know at that time that she was a schoolteacher before she met and married Ernest Woodward.

There were many discussions around the Old Brown Table about the Woodward family and, in particular, Edith and Ernest Woodward. In time these conversations would diminish, but the memories of these two exceptional individuals would last for a lifetime.

LRGN: 4-22-48; 10-8-55; 8-19-18.

Mom, Mom, I Struck Gold in the Sandbox!

In the days growing up on the farm south of Le Roy, I would spend countless hours playing in the sandbox on the west side of the farmhouse. In those days, long before computers, television, and cell phones, children would spend their fun time outdoors regardless of the weather. I remember when I was around eight years old, I would come home from school and listen to the soap operas late in the afternoon on the 1941 Philco table radio. My concerned Mom soon informed me that I was spending too much time indoors and needed to get outside for some fresh air. The Old Brown Table and I only had to hear that once because when Mom or Dad gave a command, you obeyed without question.

Well, the sandbox during the summer months was a complete joy since it would allow my imagination to be carried to many places using toys such as bright yellow metal dump trucks and front-end loaders. I would shovel the light brown sand into a mountain heap and wet it down with water so it would pack well. Then using a tablespoon, I would carve out the sand and create tunnels on two or three levels and make arched highway bridges.

One day I was carving out a mine in search of gold probably after watching the 1947 movie *"Treasure of the Sierra Madre,"* with that great Hollywood actor Humphrey Bogart. As I was hollowing out a mine shaft in the wet sand, I noticed a bright yellow object in the shape of a ring. I became very excited as I ran into the farmhouse through the back door yelling at Mom that I had struck gold in the sandbox. Unbelieving, she took the ring from my hand and washed off the brown sand under the kitchen sink faucet. The cold water washed away the sand revealing a solid gold ring. The ring had a bright finish on the inside with a 14-karat marking and a serrated finish on the outside.

That late afternoon when Dad arrived home from work around five, the Old Brown Table witnessed all the excitement I could muster when showing him the ring I had found. Dad smiled and told me it was probably a wedding ring that belonged to a Le Royan while excavating sand at the old sandpit on South Street in Le Roy. This sandpit had been around for years left by the Glaciers thousands of years ago. Dad would take two or three potato sacks, fill them with sand and deposit them in my sandbox, which measured eight by eight feet bordered by two by eight-inch pieces of construction lumber. He told me I had a ring for life since there was no way we could find the owner. I still have that ring to this day and wonder who that ring belonged to and what the man's wife said when he told her he lost his wedding ring.

Sand Box Gold Ring

My Eyes, My Eyes!

Billy was continually using the Old Brown Table for exciting projects. He loved to read the comics in the newspaper, especially the Sunday edition, when they were in color. There was Blondie, Prince Valiant, Ally Opp, Dick Tracy, Joe Palooka, Mary Worth, Popeye, Archie, Little LuLu, Gasoline Alley and of course Peanuts. With aspirations of being an inventor, Billy had the idea of cutting out the comics and placing them on a roller band so each cartoon image would appear on a screen for reading. He kept after his Dad until a device of a kind was made, which although crude worked just fine.

Then there were the high school shop projects. A wooden lamp was selected that resembled a hand water pump. When one pushed down on the pump handle, the light would be turned on or off. Most of the work was done on the Old Brown Table after newspapers were spread out to protect the table from the wood sanding, staining, and finishing.

Copper Scoop

One project was, in particular, very challenging. I was assigned in shop class to make a square scoop out of copper. The copper the shop teacher, Mr. Mangefrida, gave me was very thick and, therefore, hard to form into a small 2 by 2-inch scoop. The Old Brown Table heard a cadence of a hammer pounding the small cutout piece of copper until it resembled a small scoop. Then it needed a copper handle, so some more shaping until it became a little handle that would be soldered to the scoop. Dad did not trust me with a hot soldering iron, so he put me in charge of the round spool of solder. I watched with interest as my dad flowed the solder much like liquid silver. In my impatience, I started to whirl the two-inch spool of solder on my finger. All of a sudden, I felt an unbearable burning sensation in my eyes. The solder had a hollow core and contained acid, which served as a flux for the solder to flow evenly. When spinning the spool of solder, acid was transported from the solder into my face and eyes.

I yelled out, "My eyes, my eyes are burning!" My Dad had the presence of mind to guide me toward the sink and flush my eyes with that good ole sulfur water. There was relief at once, but the burning sensation continued, so Dad put me in the car and drove me to Le Roy to Dr. Welsh's office on West Main Street. That was the 1948 version of Urgent Care today. The doctor placed salve in my eyes and told me to continue using the ointment for the next 24 hours. As you can imagine, Dad finished the copper scoop.

Parking Meter Dilemma

After World War II, Le Roy, like many communities, was returning to a peacetime period with GI's returning home, getting jobs, and ready to raise a family. Even though there was a shortage of many items, the consumer was prepared to make purchases of cars, appliances, and other personal products. Downtown Le Roy was a hub of activity on Friday night and Saturday as the village and surrounding community residents approached Main Street stores. However, it soon became evident that there was a parking problem when you had to circle Main Street several times to find a spot. If you didn't get to Main Street early on Saturday, you would soon be frustrated before you shopped for groceries, clothes, or just wanted to take in a movie.

The village solution to this problem was parking meters, which made their Main Street debut on January 6, 1949. At first, motorists shied away from them, which resulted in making plenty of parking spaces available. However, their worth as money-makers was immediately evident to the village trustees as $20 in pennies and nickels was collected before the meters went legally into operation on January 13, 1949. Along with the real money, the citizens protested with slugs, including a Japanese coin and religious medals, which would grow with the frustration of the village residents. Mr. LaRocco,

73

the maintenance man, and collector, reported the meters to be in good working order but witnessed some distraught villagers pounding, kicking and hammering meters that did not seem to be working. He thought they should give the meters a chance after all the voters would have a say in a referendum coming in the summer.

Well, the Old Brown Table heard many a conversation over the next several months on how unfair the parking meters were to the general consumer, many of whom were from the surrounding community and would not have a vote in a village referendum. Of course, the village trustees thought parking meters would regulate the parking problem, and incidentally would bring in needed village revenue. Early in 1949, the weekly income averaged $150 ($1627 in 2020 dollars) in pennies and nickels. Motorists had a different view when they started jamming the meters with bent pennies throwing them out of commission and making it impossible for police to enforce time restrictions. Joe LaRocco was forced to remove a meter head located in front of a local grocery store four times within a week as it had been jammed with bent pennies.

Finally, the referendum date was set for May 24, 1949, for Le Roy Village voters using a single election voting machine. Since the meters had been in operation over the past five months, the take was $2581 ($28000 in 2020 dollars), with half going to the International Meter Company of Elmira and half to the village. The meter's firm take was applied to the purchase price, and the village take was split between the general fund for highways and a special fund for the purchase of a municipal parking lot.

With 374 villagers casting ballots, the vote was 249 to 122, a two to one in favor of keeping the meters. The Old Brown Table heard considerable criticism that evening. There was not one eligible voter in the house since we were outside the village limits. The village officials, along with merchants and some consumers, were jubilant since the parking problem was being managed, and the income averaging $500 per month was more than expected.

Then an incident occurred in the summer of 1949 that shook the Old Brown Table. Jack, Nellie, and Billy were hungry for an ice cream cone, so a visit was made to the Tountas Coffee Shoppe on Main Street. Jack parked in front of the Tountas store and saw the parking meter had some time left on it. The three returned to the car with ice cream in hand just as Patrolman McCarthy was writing out a ticket for a timed-out meter. Jack became rather riled and informed the zealous patrolman that they just got ice cream and were leaving. Well, that did not deter the patrolman, and he handed Jack the ticket upon which Jack abruptly turned his back and brushed the patrolman's shoulder. That was all it took for Jack to be handcuffed and marched up Main Street to the village office to face the judge. The story ended well by the judge dismissing the charge, but Jack was never able to finish his ice cream cone. That night, however, the Old Brown Table witnessed a distraught Nellie scolding Jack to have more respect for those meters.

The parking meter saga continued through the 1949 year when ticket holders were not paying the $1 fine for meter expired time. On December 8, 1949, parking violation fines neared $500 with the threat that warrants would be issued for unpaid tickets for fines up to $8. The parking meter dilemma continued for the next 35 years until, on March 1, 1984, the Le Roy Gazette reported that the parking meters would be removed. By that time, the residents had accepted the meters as just another form of village income and as a necessary part of daily life. The Old Brown Table accepted that as well!

LRGN: 1-6-49; 4-28-49; 12-4-80; 3-1-84.

Pie Plant Pete
&
Bashful Harmonica Joe

I would bet that none of you would remember the hillbilly musical duo of Pie Plant Pete and Bashful Harmonica Joe. However, the Old Brown Table remembers since it heard a lot about this pair in 1948. It was about this time when my Dad read in the Le Roy Gazette News that a hillbilly musical show was looking for an accordion player. The show was going to be held in the Le Roy High School auditorium and featured Pie Plant Pete and Bashful Harmonica Joe. The duo had a morning show on WHAM, a 50000-watt radio station in nearby Rochester. Their show played six days a week at 7:00 AM, featuring cowboy and hillbilly songs, harmonica solos, duets, clean humor with amusing imitations.

Now I was a novice accordion player since I had only taken lessons for two years from Tony Stella in Lime Rock, a crossroads two miles east of Le Roy. I had a simple 12-base accordion playing from sheet music such old songs like the Merchant of Venice and the Blue Danube waltz. I had only one song memorized, and that was the famous Beer Barrel Polka, which was loved by the local Polish and Italian community. The article in the paper said the Le Roy show needed an accordionist who could play this famous tune, and they preferred a young youth.

Now my Dad, who was now my agent, told me nothing of this until he received a call that Pie Plant Pete, the stage name for Claude Moye, wanted me in his act. When Dad gave me the news, I was frightened to death since I had never played in public before, and I honestly did not know what to expect. Well, the day came, and my parents took me to Le Roy High School, where I had just entered the middle of my seventh grade. Dad took me backstage, where I met Claude Moye, a man in his early forties dressed in a gorgeous cowboy outfit with a broad-brimmed cowboy hat. He was very kind to me and displayed a generous smile. Harmonica Joe was also present dressed in a grey suit with a funny hat and his pant legs six inches short. He also put me at ease by telling me not to be nervous since they were there to have a lot of fun, and he wanted me to join in as well. I was still not too sure of this and wanted just to go home or better yet sit in the audience and enjoy the show.

Pie Plant Pete & Bashful Joe

Pie Plant Pete then sternly instructed me that when he and I went on stage, he would play the Beer Barrel Polka on the piano in the back of me, and I would sit on a chair and play the accordion without him in sight. But then he told me the conditions under which we would play this duet. He said in no uncertain terms that I would play this famous tune all the way through without stopping regardless of what was happening in the background. Now I was warned but still did not know what to expect.

I waited nervously backstage with my Dad the minutes passing slow and sweat oozing from my hands that felt strangely cold and damp. Then I got the cue and entered the stage with Pie Plant Pete, and the accordion strapped tightly to my shoulders. After I sat down, Pete gave the cue, and we both started to play with me setting the cadence until Pete suddenly started increasing the tempo, and I was struggling to keep this rapid pace. Then the crowd started into a burst of roaring laughter that just did not stop but kept going like an approaching train coming down the track. What I could not see was Pie Plant Pete jumping up and down, making funny faces and other antics while I just played on with a straight face scared to death. When the polka ended, the crowd erupted in applause, and I just stood there beside Pete while he took the bows for us both. Offstage he told me I did just great, and later, he signed for me a copy of their songbook, "Pie Plant Pete and Bashful Joe's Favorite Old-Time Songs." I have that songbook to this day, but I don't believe I ever played a song from it since I did not favor hillbilly songs, and I did not have fond memories of that performance.

A few years later, in 1952, the duo returned for a game of Donkey Baseball in the brand-new high school gymnasium. My Dad bought tickets, but this time thank the Lord, there would be no accordion playing. Donkey Baseball was a passing phase in upstate New York and consisted of a baseball game that in no way resembled regular baseball. The local Le Roy baseball team would play, guess who, Pie Plant Pete and Bashful Harmonica Joe, and of course their prize donkey named Mildred. The game was played with Pie Plant Pete pitching the softball to Bashful Joe, the catcher. If the player at bat got a hit, he would have to hop on Mildred and gallop, or I should say shove or pull the donkey to first base. Mildred would, of course, not cooperate with any of the players until Pete and Joe came up to bat, and Mildred would respond with their every command. You now know who won the game, Pie Plant Pete and Bashful Harmonica Joe.

Now seventy years have passed, and I lost complete track of Pete and Joe except now and then have that distant memory of the incident in 1948. So, to obtain background information on this little-known

Pete and Joe duo, I Googled it, and to my surprise, I discovered they became very well known as Country/Hillbilly song artists. Pete or Claude Moye was a profound musical influence on Les Paul, who was several years younger than Claude. Claude prompted Les Paul into a professional path leading to Paul's invention of the electric guitar and multi-track recording. He later became famous as an American jazz, country and blues guitarist, songwriter and inventor.

Now Pete and Joe started as a duo after separate careers in the country/hillbilly music arena. Pete met Joe in Cleveland, Ohio, in 1936, where they teamed up with the famous names of Pie Plant Pete and Bashful Harmonica Joe. It was a good match since Pete took on the straight man and Joe was the comic. They were good songwriters accompanied with great lyrics. Although World War II interrupted their act for five years, they got back together in 1946 with daily performances on WHAM in Rochester, NY. The WHAM shows lead to local concerts in auditoriums around the upstate New York area, including Le Roy in 1948 and 1951. They performed at several major radio stations such as WJW (Cleveland), WSPD (Toledo), WTAM (Cleveland), WBZ (Boston), WSYR (Syracuse), and WHAM (Rochester). They wrote many songs throughout their careers such as, "There's a Rocking Chair Waiting in Heaven," "When You're In Love," "I'm Blazin A Trail To Paradise," and "Down By The Railroad Tracks." They usually ended their radio show with the song, "I'll Remember Your Love in My Prayers."

The Old Brown Table and Le Roy, for that matter, never realized what a famous duo they hosted at Le Roy High School in the Spring of 1948!

Ref: Hillbilly-Music.com – Pie Plant Pete and Bashful Harmonica Joe

Red Ryder Run

On July 5, 1941, Billy had a very close call with his Red Ryder wagon. Only six years old, he would play in the driveway with his Red Ryder moving his imaginary cargo from one place to the other or placing his left knee in the wagon and pushing with his right leg. The boyhood activity was all good fun for a young boy that used his imagination to the fullest.

On a warm sunny Saturday morning, all seemed usual with Billy enjoying a warm July 4th weekend. All of a sudden, a car pulled into the driveway out of control. The car was swerving from side to side up the driveway heading right for Billy. Fortunately, he had the presence of mind to jump out of his wagon and head for the backdoor of the house. He barely reached the back door when the car crashed into the Red Ryder with a thud driving the wagon up against the concrete support for the basement door. Dad and Mom were in the kitchen by the Old Brown Table when they heard the crash and ran for the back door, not sure what had happened.

Billy was standing on the back doorsteps with a frightened look on his face. He stared at the Red Ryder that was bent in half crushed between the basement door and the bumper of a car. A couple from Buffalo, NY, by the name of Ray and Louise Marr, got out of the vehicle frightened just like Billy. Ray was distraught with his wife, who had lost control when she turned into our country home driveway coming from the south direction. He quickly explained that he was teaching Louise to drive on their journey from Buffalo to Le Roy, and all was going well until they reached their destination.

After the excitement was over and Billy was sadly viewing his immobile prize wagon, Louise said they would buy him a new one, which helped boost Billy's moral. As the weeks and months went by, however, a new Red Ryder wagon never showed up, so Dad banged out the damage, and the crinkled wagon was again back in action with Billy at the controls. Red Ryder was on the move again!

Religion & White Sand

As a young boy, I attended a one-room schoolhouse named District #11, located on Cole Road in Jug City close to the O-At-Ka Creek. Can you believe the name Jug City, which was named after its only industry in history, that is making jugs for whatever reason? District #11 was my school for the next seven and a half years until the middle of the seventh grade. When I reached third grade my parents were told I would have to attend Christian Doctrine classes held on Monday afternoon at our local church in Le Roy. The Le Roy Wolcott Street School and Le Roy High School would let out early on Monday, around 2 PM for students to attend religion classes at various churches in town. Students would walk from the public school to the church since the distance was less than a mile. For my parents this created a problem since District #11 located in Jug City was four miles from the church in town.

Le Roy Plow Works Foundry

So, my parents found a man that worked second shift at the Lapp Insulator that would provide me a ride from the Jug City school to the plant, and from there, I would walk the remainder of the distance about one mile to the church on Lake Street. As a young boy, I did not mind walking the distance, whether in the mild Fall or frigid Winter. After the religion class, I would walk a short distance through a back unpaved road to the rear of the Le Roy Plow Works, where Dad worked as an iron molder in the foundry.

There were no restrictions in those days upon entering a factory, and I had the liberty of walking anywhere I wanted in the plant. I was fascinated watching a large coal-fired steam engine with a 10-foot diameter flywheel power eight-inch wide belts to overhead driveshafts, which in turn powered various machines throughout the plant. Nowadays, all machines are powered by electric motors eliminating these hazardous unguarded belts from catching clothing, etc. My father told me that a man was caught in one of these belts, and it took his arm off, and that taught me to keep my distance from these spinning machines.

Now the foundry where my Dad worked was the most dangerous place since a large six-foot diameter bucket would bring molten iron, heated in a coke-fired cupula to the sand molds prepared by the molder each morning. The molds were primarily for farm plow blades and points, although parts for other farm implements were molded as well. The heat from the orange molten iron would scorch your face, and the smell of the iron and coke would fill your nostrils. After pouring the hot molten iron in the molds, the molder would wait a few hours for the iron to harden before breaking apart the sand molds and releasing into view the birth of a heavy cast iron piece. The sand was then heaped into a long row about 12-feet long in preparation for the next day. Each molder had his row in the foundry with enough space for about 20 molders.

One day when I arrived through the back door, my Dad was just breaking apart the molds, and the hot cast iron would send up rays of heat into the large room that felt like an oven. No heat was required in this large room in the winter due to the heat from the molten metal. Sweat would pour from the molder's forehead and arms as he performed his duties in this very strenuous work. This particular day the molder next to my Dad broke apart his molds, and almost all of his cast-iron product was defective. Dad gave me a lesson on "haste makes waste" since this molder did not take sufficient time to prepare his molds.

I did not like to stay in the foundry room very long since it was always uncomfortably hot, dusty, and very noisy so, I would go out the back door and walk through rows of molding boxes looking for treasure. On such a trek, I came across a large bin full of white sand glistening in the sun, which I thought was quite appealing since I was only used to my brown sandbox sand. On the backside of this large bin, there was a hole in the box which allowed a large amount of white sand to pour onto the ground. On viewing this great escape of sand, I ran into the foundry and announced to my Dad that I had discovered this unusual leak of sand into the environment. He calmly told me he would get the plant manager, and we would check out this large sand leak.

As soon as the day shift ended, my Dad, the plant manager Tom Larkin and I led the way to the white sand leak. I felt so important that I had discovered this problem and thought maybe I would be rewarded in some way. Instead, my Dad and Tom Larkin had a good laugh since this apparent bin failure would not impact production or create a plant crisis as my imagination envisioned.

The Old Brown Table heard a lot of laughter at the dinner table that evening on the mix of religion and white sand!

LRGN: 7-3-29; 12-18-29; 3-3-49.

Richard Longhany Is Missing

On April 22, 1943, the first war tragedy to strike our extended family occurred. Nellie Brown was sitting at the Old Brown Table, writing a letter to her son Frank when a cousin stopped by with some distressing news. Nellie's sister Lucy Longhany just received a telegram from the War Department that her son was "missing in action, somewhere at sea." Peter and Lucy Longhany lived in Lime Rock, NY, just a few miles East of Le Roy. They had three boys and three girls. Richard, the oldest, was 21 and had enlisted in the Navy on August 22, 1942. He became Seaman First Class and trained at the Great Lakes Naval Training Station, Armory Gunnery School in Chicago, IL. In February 1943, he was serving as a gunner on the merchant ship Jonathan Sturges in convoy in the North Atlantic.

Seaman First Class Richard Longhany

American merchant ships were supplying England and other Allies such as Russia with vital war materials produced in the USA. Germany, at this time, had developed an extensive submarine fleet to sink these ships wherever they were sighted.

On the night of February 23, 1943, two torpedoes without warning hit Richard's ship. Onboard, the Jonathan Sturges were 22 US Navy armed guards and a ship crew of 29. The German sub after surfacing took as prisoners' two Navy armed guards and four of the ship's crew. Richard never made it to the lifeboats, and his family was told later that his death was definite. Eddy Longhany, Richard's brother, talked to one of the survivors that lived in Connecticut. The survivor told Eddy that he hid in the darkness from the Germans since he did not want to be taken as a prisoner of war. He survived on a raft in the frigid North Atlantic for eleven days and was very fortunate to be picked up by another convoy. Now that decision took an incredible amount of courage!

Peter and Lucy Longhany were not notified until two months after the sinking, on April 22, 1943, that he was missing in action. It wasn't until a year later, February 1944, when they were notified that his ship had been torpedoed on February 23, 1943. They waited for an entire year with the hope that their son was alive, maybe in a German prison camp. Richard N. Longhany was awarded the American and European Campaign Medals, and Purple Heart for giving his life for his country.

Little did Jack and Nellie Brown realize that in a little over a year, in mid-1944, they would face the same tragedy of not knowing the fate of their son Frank. These were sad and tragic days witnessed by the Old Brown Table.

Salmon on Ice With 1720 Wine

My brother Al and I did a lot of fishing at Conesus Lake and some on Lake Ontario. Dad and Al built a 16-foot wooden boat that was a Sears & Roebuck kit, including the trailer to haul the boat to lake or stream. The boat was very well constructed, but the trailer was too flimsy for the boat since the axle kept breaking where it attached to the wheel. The failure was not a good thing when traveling down the road, and suddenly, you see a trailer wheel traveling past you in a farmer's field. This unfortunate event occurred upon returning from fishing at Lake Ontario near Hamlin Beach. Dad borrowed a long bed pickup truck from his employer Charles Metcalf to pick up the boat and trailer with the broken axle.

I wish I could report that the fishing was successful, but unfortunately, we seldom brought home any fish. We tried everything with lures and bait, but nothing seemed to work to catch those smart fish. Even trolling and deep-water fishing up to 80 feet at Seneca Lake did not produce results. Well, the adventure was fun, regardless, and the challenge always present.

In mid-1947, my dad received a gift from Ernest Woodward with whom he was employed as the master gardener on the East Main Popular Lane Farm estate. Ernest was an avid sportsman, and in 1947 he traveled to Alaska for a hunting and fishing expedition. Before he returned to Le Roy, his employees and friends starting receiving fresh whole salmon crated in ice. Dad got his salmon when a Railway Express delivery truck arrived at our house with a wooden crate about four feet long. The box was opened with excitement on the Old Brown Table, and therein packed in ice was the most beautiful salmon you could ever imagine. My eyes could not believe the size of this fish glistening under the ice. It was a Sockeye salmon about 30 inches long.

Well, in the next few days, our family devoured that beautiful fish. In 1947 the price of fresh salmon was far too high for our family to purchase. Fresh seafood was not available like it is today in the local markets. I remember my mom fixing salted codfish taken from a small six-inch wooden box. She would soak it in water first to remove the salt and then cook it with milk and flour. I did not like it very much, which provided me with a disdained outlook on seafood.

Working for Ernest Woodward had many rewards since he was very appreciative and generous to his employees. We always received a turkey for Thanksgiving and Christmas, making our table grand indeed. Now Ernest had a well-stocked wine cellar in the basement of the mansion. One day Dad was summoned by Ernest and was handed an old dusty bottle of wine. He told dad that the date on the label, which was very hard to read, was 1720, and he did not want to drink it for fear he might become sick. Ernest jokingly told Dad he would like him to try it, and if he did not become ill, he had a case in the wine cellar that would be his. Well, Dad took it home, and I was astonished at the age of the bottle. You could barely make out the label and date. We watched as dad removed the cork, which was severely deteriorated. Dad poured out a small glass and took a sip immediately followed by spitting it out in the sink by the Old Brown

Table. Vinegar, he shouted! Air had entered the bottle many years before and had turned the wine to vinegar.

As you would imagine Dad did not ask for the remaining case in the Woodward wine cellar!

Skiing is Fun, but Skating is Worse

On a cold winter day in 1945, I was bored with the long, endless winter and started looking for things to do on my Christmas vacation. I ventured up into the barn loft, where years back, hay was stored for the horse and cow, which for several years were no longer present on the small farm. The loft now had become an attic for storing those items that were no longer needed in the house proper. I usually would find something interesting, and on this cold day, I came upon a pair of skis most probably used by my older brothers. My immediate thought was to put these skis to use since we had a large hill a quarter mile to the west of our farm.

Now there were several inches of snow on the ground from a recent snowfall, so with glee and a new sense of adventure, I took the skis from the barn, brushed off several years of dust, and brought them to the farmhouse. I found a can of Johnsons Wax and meticulously brushed on a thick coat of wax. If I was going to try skiing, I certainly wanted to achieve as fast a speed as was possible. After this waxing and polishing, I proudly brought the skis to the kitchen, where the Old Brown Table heard my exciting upcoming adventure. My mom cautioned me to be careful since skiing to her was synonymous with breaking an arm or a leg. Well, not me, I exclaimed, since I would be very cautious.

I put on my winter coat, scarf, gloves, a hat with earmuffs, and with the skis on my shoulder started on my adventure. I took a shortcut through the field to Cole Road and then west up the road, which after crossing the B&O railroad tracks, gradually took a gradual climb up a hill. Upon reaching the summit, I entered the field, which had been harvested for hay in the fall and had a six-inch covering of fluffy snow. I strapped on my newly polished skis and gazed in excitement to the intense fall ahead of me. Indeed, I will reach maximum speed with Johnson Wax and be able to tell all my friends about my skiing ability. Now what I did not think about was the need for poles to steady or change direction. Also, stopping was neither considered.

With my shoes in the leather straps, I moved my body forward, heading down the hill. To my surprise, I quickly picked up speed, and a sense of exhilaration flowed through my veins, followed by a sudden sense of terror. My mom's caution now was going over and over in my mind as my speed increased. Suddenly I realized I was headed for a grove of trees at the bottom of the hill. How can I avoid the trees, slow down, or for heaven's sake stop! Now, in panic mode and accelerating faster and faster, I made a critical decision. Just plain and simple, sit down on my rear end, and the result was a gradual stop with me covered with that white fluffy snow.

Billy With Skis

After a minute or two, I pulled my feet from the leather straps, got up, and placed the skis on my shoulder and made a quick trip home. The skis went back to the barn loft, ready for the next adventurous person. I related to the family around the Old Brown Table that evening that this was just too much adventure for a ten-year-old boy. I would try ice skating since I was sure it would be much better. So, the next day back to the barn loft, I went, and surprisingly, I found four sets of ice skates. I tried them all on until I found the right fit and told Mom I would check the ice the next day on the small stream behind our farm.

Now in the fall, the Johnson milk farm had hired an excavator to deepen the creek that crossed Cole Road by the B&O Railroad tracks right up to where it entered our farm property. The next day I ventured down to the small stream and discovered it was completely covered with ice. With glee and excitement, I ran back home and picked up my ice skates for a new adventure. When I told Mom where I was going, she cautioned me to be careful and make sure the ice was thick enough to hold my weight.

Within ten minutes, I sat on the bank of the small creek and put on my skates. The stream was at least ten feet wide covered with bright glistening ice. I started down the ice with a new sense of adventure. Ice cold air entered my nostrils as I pushed left, right, left, right, and then coasted for a distance. Skating was much better than skiing, and I could coast to a stop any time I wanted to. It was a beautiful day and thought I was in heaven with this new sport. All of a sudden, I heard a strange sound on the ice beneath me, a cracking sound that is. To my horror, I saw the ice crack right down the middle of the ten-foot-wide ice-covered creek, and almost immediately, water came seeping up through the long break. That was enough for me as I hurried to the side, leaped up, and fell on the snow-covered bank. That was it! The water continued to ooze through and slowly covered the ice.

Off to home, I went accepting the fact that ice skating along with skiing was not for me as well. Well, the Old Brown Table did not hear that story at dinner because my Dad or Mom would never trust me again with these ambitious adventures.

Smoking 49 Chevy

In the late 1940s, Dad got the urge for a new car. During World War Two, from 1941 to 1945, private car production was stopped with all production directed to support the war effort. It took some time for the car manufacturers to make the transition back to the private and commercial consumers. During the late 1940s, inflation was also running at a high rate, which made a car purchase all the more painful. Regardless my Dad and Mom decided in late 1948 to purchase a new car. You had to place an order for a car since there were no new car lots where you could view cars and pick out the one you wanted to negotiate a price. Well, there was no negotiation at all since the demand was far greater than supply.

Dad ordered a two-door 1949 Chevy with a six-cylinder engine. He said two doors were better than four since there were fewer doors to rattle. The V-8 cylinder engines were just emerging at the time and were unreliable due to many mechanical problems. At this time, Edgar J. Hudson opened a new Chevrolet dealership on January 23, 1949, on Main Street called Le Roy Motors. One day in April, Dad received notice that the car had arrived. At the Old Brown Table, Dad asked me to accompany him to the dealership to pick up the vehicle. When we arrived, Dad found out that the price had increased since there were now fog-lights on the front bumper and rear fender panels covering the back wheels, which had not been ordered. In those days, you took what you got and didn't ask questions.

Dad had cash in hand, and we went upstairs to Edgar Hudson's brand-new office. When dad was given a fountain ink pen to sign the paper, he could not get the pen to write, so he quickly gave the pen a downward jerk to get the ink to flow. Well, it flowed all right when it gushed out on Mr. Hudson's brand-new office floor. I was so embarrassed, and I believe my Dad was as well. Mr. Hudson didn't seem to mind as he went to get a towel to wipe up the ink.

Dad drove out of that dealership, a proud owner of a new car, which commanded attention since there were very few new cars on the road. We went home, and at the Old Brown Table invited everyone to ride the new car for the first time. It was a cold, cloudy day the week before Easter, and Dad drove south on Route 19 toward Pavilion. The vehicle rode so smoothly, and one could hardly hear the engine running. Dad kept the speed to less than forty miles per hour since, in those days, you had to break in the engine at a lower speed for a few thousand miles. At some point, Dad came to a stop, and we smelled something burning. He got out of the car to investigate this smell and discovered the back brakes were smoking. With horror, he found out he had not completely released the parking brake before leaving home. The slight drag on the brakes caused overheating of the brake lining, which was smoking with a dreadful odor. There was nothing we could do but wait a while for the rear brakes to cool off and then return home.

Not a good beginning for a new car but not a disaster either. However, as witnessed by the Old Brown Table, the joy in having a new vehicle overshadowed all.

LRGN: 1-20-49.

St. Joe's Call Back

In the Roman Catholic Church, when you reach the age of nine, you are required to make your first Holy Communion after receiving instruction from the Confraternity of Christian Doctrine classes. At this time, the family was attending St. Joseph's Church on Lake Street in Le Roy, which is where I received my religious instruction on the Mass, commandments, and the traditions of the church. I was nine years old when the date was set in April 1945. World War II was still in process against Japan in the South Pacific, although the war in Germany was soon coming to an end. Americans were growing weary of the war due to the loss of so many young servicemen. Goods and services had become very restricted due to the priority given to the war effort.

Before receiving your first communion, you were required to make your first confession. The nuns taught us how to do a mental examination of your past sins, which would then be confessed to a priest. There were two classes of sins, venial and mortal. A mortal sin was the most serious, and you were told an unconfessed mortal sin would send you straight to Hell. The nuns were masters at putting the fear of God into us to where I dreaded making this first confession in a dark closet structure located in the church sanctuary. The confessional housed a priest in the center, and there were usually two doors on either side where a person could enter. At St. Joe's due to limitations of space, there was only a single confessional which housed a priest in a cubical and an adjacent cubical for the confessing person. There was a screen separating the priest from the confessor so you could converse and remain anonymous. On the outside, there was a green light that indicated a priest was present and a red light when a person was in the confessional to show it was occupied.

When the day came, I was terrified and not sure of what sins I should confess, how many or how many times. The nuns marched us, boys and girls, into the church and lined us up in a single file before the confessional. We waited until the priest, Father Ormsby, came in and entered the confessional illuminating the red light. We were alphabetical in line, so I waited my turn after the first A's and B's made their confession.

Now my family knew Father Ormsby since my sister Eleanor worked part-time as a housekeeper at the parsonage next door to the church. I remember accompanying my Dad to pick up Eleanor after a day of cleaning, and we sometimes would be invited by Father Ormsby to enter the parsonage. Father Ormsby was a young, outspoken priest who pulled no punches, so when he greeted my Dad, he asked, "Jack, do you want a shot?". Now that was not a shot of holy water, but the real thing! I was offered a glass of orange juice accompanied by a large peanut butter cookie that the cook just took out of the oven. Now we always had homemade cookies at home but never had orange juice since it was considered a luxury. I remember eating that cookie as slow as I could with that glass of orange juice to make it last as long as possible.

Billy First Communion

Entering the confessional, I knelt down and informed Father Ormsby my three venial sins. He started his routine, asking God to forgive my sins, so I thought I was finished and immediately left the confessional. I got out of there as fast as a nine-year-old boy could accomplish. When I was halfway down the aisle, passing those that were still waiting to confess, to my horror the priest opened his door and yelled, "Hey, you there, get back in here, you are not finished yet!" Well, I could have melted on the spot, but stopped dead in my tracks and retreated to the confessional with Father Ormsby watching. What had I done? The answer was I had left too quickly before the priest had absolved me and given my penance of three Our Fathers and three Hail Mary's. When I left the confessional the second time, I got quite a few stares from the remaining boys and girls probably with terror in their heart of what they, in turn, were facing.

Well, that evening, dinner at the Old Brown Table heard of my embarrassing experience, which drew laughter from my sister and brother but only comfort and consolation from Mom.

Strike at Lapp Insulator

One of the largest employers in Le Roy was the Lapp Insulator company on Gilbert Street, with a workforce of around 700 employees in the 1950s. The company produced electrical insulators of all types and sizes for the electrical power industry and shipped their product around the world. Just a few years after World War II in late 1947, there was general discord among the workers primarily concerning wages. Due to the nation's monetary policy and the industry conversion from wartime to peacetime production, the inflation rate increased dramatically. In late 1946 and early 1947, the inflation rate was around 13 to 19%, which caused great concern with the factory worker seeing very little increase in their wages, and the prices of goods and services increase dramatically.

The Lapp Insulator production workers were represented by the American Federation of Labor Workers, who wanted a union shop at the plant. The union contract was about to expire by mid-1948, so negotiations were started early centered around a union demand of an increase of 10 cents per hour wage and a union shop. A union shop, by definition, is a company in which the employer, by agreement, is free to hire union members and nonmembers but keeps nonunion members on the payroll only on condition of their becoming members of the union within a specified time. In other words, all production workers are required to be members of the union. The negotiations went on for weeks without resolution until the workers walked off their job on March 19, 1948, causing all production to cease.

Almost every week, management and union met to resolve the strike with picketing occurring outside the plant on a 24-hour basis. The union representing the employees stayed fast on their demand of 10 cents per hour increase and a union shop with the management offering 7 cents per hour increase but no union shop. In the spring of 1948, the days and weeks went by with no resolution causing this to be the most prolonged and most bitter strike in Le Roy history with a significant effect on the general economy in Le Roy.

Finally, the strike was settled on Sunday, May 6, 1948, with all employees back to work by May 17. Management agreed to an hourly increase in wages of 9 cents per hour but no union shop. Lapp did increase holiday and a few other benefits. The Old Brown Table heard a lot of discussions over the seven week strike mainly since some relatives worked at the Lapp plant. More than once, my Dad would explain that the workers were losing more than gaining caused by their seven-week wage loss. His Lapp relatives having their pride and pocketbook affected thought otherwise. Who knows what the Old Brown Table thought!

LRGN: 4-8,15,22,29-1948; 5-6-1948.

Swimming at the Ole Swimming Hole

Many of us have memories of our favorite swimming hole where we would escape the summer heat in a refreshing pool of cold water. There was a gravel pit about a half-mile south of the old farmhouse very close to the abandoned salt mine that offered a perfect place to swim. When my cousins would visit, we would hop on our bikes, and in a few minutes, we were swimming in cold clear water.

On one occasion, I was invited by one of my cousins to swim at the General Crushed Stone quarry about two miles north of Lime Rock. The quarry was enormous, which had been in use for many years. There was a large pond of water in the abandoned section of the quarry that offered not only water but rocks where you could jump off into deep water. An adult never supervised us at these locations, and it is a wonder that we did not experience an accident. However, on returning home that hot summer afternoon, I became very ill, and this puzzled my parents since there was no flu going around, especially during the summer months. My cousins, who were swimming with me, became ill as well. So, my Mom, after some investigation with their mothers, found out the dire cause. The water was polluted since somebody and dumped a dead pig in the water. Now can you believe that a person would be that irresponsible? The Old Brown Table heard the sad, or I should say the sick story that evening while I was absent from the dinner table. We all learned a lesson that day to never swim at that location again.

Nowadays, communities have public swimming pools, but Le Roy was too small a village to afford such a luxury. They did run school buses during the summer months to Horseshoe Lake just north of Stafford, NY, for the summer recreation program. I did not care for that swimming hole because there were just too many kids in too small a place.

One year there was a shortage of rain, and the gravel pit became too shallow and polluted with algae. So, a boyfriend and I decided to try Beaver Meadow one mile south of the old farmhouse and just south of the abandoned salt mine. We hiked down the B&O railroad tracks until we reached the meadow, which was at least a half-mile across and filled with cattails immersed in freshwater. Just off

Ray & Billy At Ole Swimming Hole

the railroad tracks, there was a large pool of water where we decided to swim. As soon as we waded into the water, our feet sunk six inches into the muck, that is rich mud. You could barely move, so I tried to swim a small distance until I came eye to eye with a water snake. Well, that took care of that swimming hole, and with frustration, we evacuated immediately. The Old Brown Table heard quite a story that night.

The favorite swimming hole without question was Hamlin Beach State Park. After I complained about our local swimming experience, my parents started taking me to Hamlin Beach on Lake Ontario. Mom would pack a picnic dinner, including homemade potato salad, hot dogs, hamburgers, macaroni salad, and don't forget the cookies. Usually, we would take two cars since relatives and friends would join the Sunday trip. It was about 30-miles to the park on the shores of Lake Ontario, traveling north on Route 19. I remember I was usually impatient and just could not wait to get to the lake water. First, we would have the picnic feast at one of the many picnic tables. The shelters were constructed of beautiful red flagstone and offered charcoal-fired grills for the dogs and hamburgers. After the picnic feast, I was ready for the beach and water but was always told I would have to wait an hour before entering the water. That was the most extended hour I can ever remember.

The lake breeze was so enticing along with the lake water aroma entering your nostrils that made the experience well worth the 30-mile drive. Usually, there was an offshore breeze, and I would love the waves moving up onto the beach. On one occasion, we had an inflated beach ball, and on that particular day, there was a strong breeze that carried the ball rapidly out to the lake. My brother Al demonstrated his swimming talent when before the Lifeguard could say stop, he vaulted forward and, in a few minutes, retrieved the ball and returned it to us.

On returning home, the Old Brown Table would hear what an exhilarating day it was at the beach, and we could not wait until next Sunday to experience it again.

The Loss of a High School Classmate

The final days of 1950 brought tragedy to the Le Roy High School sophomore class with a horrific auto accident that took the life of classmate Kay Francis Hungerford, 15 years old. The Old Brown Table, on the evening of December 28, 1950, heard the details of the horrific accident that took one life and seriously injured five others. Dad overheard the injured girls screamed and cried with pain for over an hour. They were pinned in the wreckage and had to be cut out of the twisted metal. These were the days when seat belts were not yet on the drawing board, and the Jaws of Life, a hydraulic extraction tool, was not invented until 1961, eleven years later.

The auto accident occurred near the Le Roy Golf Course at about 2:30 pm Friday when a car driven by Mrs. Marion Daniels of South Street, traveling east on East Main road, went out of control and struck a westbound tractor-trailer head-on. Kenneth Stoll, uninjured, was operating the tractor-trailer owned by the Buffalo Septic Tank Company and heavily loaded with concrete septic tanks. Slippery road conditions between Le Roy and Caledonia were believed to have been responsible for Mrs. Daniels's loss of control, which sent the car into the path of the tractor-trailer. The impact of the collision jack-knifed the truck, and the mangled car was shoved off the south side of the road.

The car was so severely damaged that the injured could not be rescued until the arrival of acetylene cutters from the Le Roy Department of Public Works and the nearby Kunego Welding Service. The extraction of injured was delayed for almost one hour until placed in ambulances from St. Jerome and Genesee Memorial Hospitals.

Kay Francis Hungerford, 15, daughter of Burton M. Hungerford of Griswold road, suffered a broken neck and fractured skull and was taken to St. Jerome Hospital, where she died at 12:08 am. Saturday. Seriously injured were Mrs. Daniels, who sustained chest and back injuries and a possible fractured left leg; her daughter Betty Jane, 13, with a broken left leg and Beverly, 15, a fractured right leg. Sandra Hutchison of Maple Avenue, suffered less severe injuries with head lacerations and Jean Lang, 17, of Wolcott street with multiple abrasions and body bruises.

The High School Sophomore class was stunned when they returned to school in January 1951 with the loss of Kay Hungerford and the severe injury to Beverly Daniels. The hallways of the high school witnessed Beverly on crutches for several weeks with her classmates wishing her a quick recovery. However, the knowledge that we would never see Kay again, that she would never walk down the graduation aisle, never be married and have a family, stayed with the Class of 53 for the remaining high school years.

LRGN: 12-28-1950.

The Red Cross Letter

On the morning of June 6, 1944, which today is named D-Day, Mom wrote her son at the Old Brown Table, *"This morning I tuned in on the radio about eight o'clock and heard the news of the invasion. I listened all day as time seemed to stand still. Tonight, we all went to church at St. Peters, and there was a large crowd. Father McCoy said for all to pray more every day that world peace will come soon. We were thinking something was up as no one is getting mail from England. I pray and hope you won't have to leave England, but if you do, I pray God will watch over you and bring you back home safe again. I hope this will end the war sooner now. Dad, Alfred and Eleanor, and all employees got a half-hour off from work today to go to church. Billy said he prayed for you on his way to the school this morning. Will close now and say my prayers and then get to bed. Love from us all and loads from Mother."*

Nellie's son Frank W. Brown had entered the army on May 15, 1941, and after three years of training in the 4th Infantry, 12th Regiment, he was deployed from England on the greatest naval invasion in world history. She, like most mothers, knew that he was likely a part of this invasion, which was indeed true. Due to a high level of secrecy and strict censorship, loved ones back home did not know the plan for Operation Overlord, the invasion of France to defeat Germany.

As the days slowly rolled by in June, there was a long agonizing period where Mom, Dad, and the family did not know anything about Frank. First, if indeed he was in the invasion, where was he at this time? Second, was he wounded or even worse captured by the Germans and now held as a prisoner of war? They could not believe the very worst had happened since they would have been notified within a few days if he had been severely injured or killed. No one feared, worried, and agonized more than Mom, and her primary reaction was to pray throughout the day and write more letters at least every other day. Indeed, the letters must be getting through to him.

Then on July 1, 1944, a letter was received from Pfc. Al MacDonald (Mac), with a Red Cross letterhead dated June 24, 1944. Al MacDonald was in Frank's squad and was severely wounded on June 9. He was recovering now in a hospital in England and wrote this letter thinking that Frank's parents had already been notified of their son's death. As it turned out, this was the first notification of anything wrong and only resulted in disbelief and more confusion. Mac, with good intentions, was trying to express his grief in the loss of such a close personal friend. A year later Mac sincerely regretted sending this letter as he spoke to Frank's parents and others.

Pfc. Al MacDonald writes, *"Words cannot express my feelings on the recent loss of your son and my pal Frank. As you know, we had much in common, therefore, our friendship was a continual affair. Frank was a most conservative fellow, and like myself, we both didn't smoke and drink. We found our pleasures in the movies of which we went but often. Our day would compose of a movie and ice cream, southern fried chicken, and more ice cream. We sure did like our ice cream, and often we'd boast as to how much we could eat. I told him of a place in Hartford Conn. called the Highland Dairy, where they had super sundaes and wagered Frank a bet that he couldn't eat one of their Steamboats. I was quickly accepted on this challenge, so time was to tell. It makes me sad to reminisce like this, but how can I ever forget such a swell pal. Of how we often spoke of our plans and how we were both expected to visit one another. As he stated, I'll show you all around Le Roy to which I used to reply that won't take long. They come no better than Frank, and I'm saying this from a fellow speaking from the heart. He kept up exceptionally well on his religious duties, which was just another fine point about him. Yes, Frank and I had much in common, and someday with your permission, I'd like to meet the parents of this pal of mine. Frank left memories with the people in whom he came in contact with and me. He was happy and carefree in life, and when the final whistle blew at the end of his day, I'm certain that he entered the Great Beyond with just as much enthusiasm and hope for the future. Yes, Mr. and Mrs. Brown, he was indeed a fine young man. A pal of Franks, Al MacDonald."*

I remember this day well, a bright and sunny day on Saturday, July 1, 1944. The family was all home except for Mary, who was in Rochester, working at Eastman Kodak. It was around noon, and the mailman had come with the morning mail. Mom would usually walk down the driveway to get the mail, and she would wait anxiously to see if there were any letters from Frank. There had not been any letters for about two weeks now, the last being dated May 31. We all gathered in the kitchen around the Old Brown Table to hear the news. Dad, Mom, Al, Eleanor, and I waited for Mom to open the letter and read it. Since it was on a Red Cross letterhead, there was an obvious concern. When my Mom read that first line, "Words cannot express my feelings on the recent loss of your son and my pal Frank," she burst out in tears with "Oh my God, Oh my God!" My father was smoking a pipe and threw it across the kitchen floor, hitting it so hard it broke into two pieces. My brother Al started to cry and ran out the back door and down the field past the red barn. Eleanor tried to comfort Mom in total shock of what had just been made known. I just stood there, a boy of almost nine years, shocked and just not knowing what to do in such grief, which I had never experienced before in my life. I'm not sure of the rest of that fateful day, but what I do know is that my parents could not believe that Frank was dead since there was no official confirmation from the War Department. Two months later, the last news was received from the War Department that Sgt. Frank W. Brown was killed in action on June 13, 1944, which was later corrected to June 8, 1944.

There were thirty-one letters written by his mother to Frank from May 26 to August 4, 1944. These letters were never answered but held somewhere by the army during this period. All 31 letters were returned at the same time in mid-August, and each was marked, "Return to Sender, Deceased," signed, and dated by the platoon officer, Lt. William A. Forbes.

The Fateful Telegram

The Brown Family waited it seemed forever to hear any news that Staff/Sgt. Frank W. Brown was alive. The Red Cross letter received on July 1, 1944, from PFC Al MacDonald, who served in Frank's platoon, caused somber doubts that he was alive, but since no official word had been received from the War Department, there was hope.

Upon receiving the Red Cross letter, Billy recalls seeing his mother grief-stricken sitting at the Old Brown Table. She called her sister Lucy

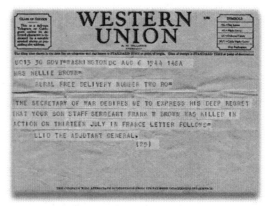

War Department Telegram

who immediately came over to comfort her. Billy had a difficult time seeing his Mom in tears and remembers going out of the house to his swing hung from the apple tree near the front yard. Aunt Lucy was at this time, also dealing with the grief of the loss of her son Richard Longhany. Richard was a Navy gunner on the merchant ship Jonathan Sturges in convoy crossing the Atlantic, which was torpedoed on the night of February 23, 1943, as noted previously in this book. His parents were notified on April 22, 1943, that he was missing at sea, but were not officially notified until February 24, 1944, a year after his death. What a long, long time, his parents waited, not knowing if he survived as a prisoner of war. So, these two grief-stricken sisters were a comfort to each other at this very trying time. Billy remembers Aunt Lucy as a very kind and caring woman who displayed a concerned and anxious look on her face. How can a person live a grief experience such as this without it affecting them in many different ways?

On August 6, 1944, a Western Union telegram was delivered to the Brown homestead on Pavilion Road. It was addressed to Mrs. Nellie Brown, Rural Free Delivery Number Two, and read, "The Secretary of War desires me to express his deep regret that your son Staff Sergeant Frank W. Brown was killed in action on Thirteen July in France. Letter follows. The Adjutant General." When it was read at the Old Brown Table, it ended all remaining hope the family had of Frank being alive. As the following year passed, Billy witnessed many times his mother sobbing as she tried to prepare dinner around the Old Brown Table.

Frank's father took the grief differently. He was a hardworking, very kind man with strong character. However, as a man, he had trouble handling grief, and it showed right away in anger. He was angry at the War Department for taking so long to get a reply. He was irritated when they found out the date of death, as called out on the August 6th telegram, was not June 13 but instead June 8. He was angry when he read in the newspapers that many times the men were not protected by tanks or armored vehicles but would have to expose themselves entirely to the enemy to gain ground. He knew the 4th Division was initially designed as a rolling armored division where the tanks and half-tracs were embedded in the various companies, but this changed in late 1943. He was angry at the President and Congress for being responsible for the greatest nation in the world being unprepared for the war and suffering such a defeat at Pearl Harbor. This anger was expressed many a time at the Old Brown Table, and Billy was sure not to question or challenge him.

Shortly after the August 6th telegram, Billy remembers being in the town of Le Roy with his father riding in the 1936 Chevy four-door sedan. We pulled up in front of the Le Roy Municipal Building. In front of the building was a sizable billboard, around 8 feet high and 18 feet long. On it were the names of Le Roy WWII servicemen and women, each painted on a 2 by 12-inch board, nailed to the billboard. Those killed had a gold star by the name. Billy's father left the car with a pair of pliers and tore off Frank's name, rushed back to the car, and quickly put it under the driver's floor mat. Billy was shocked and thought we are in trouble, and the police will soon be after us. That did not happen, of course, and Billy never told anyone about what happened that day, not even the Old Brown Table. That was a father's way of handling his grief.

Undulant Fever

In late spring 1941, my sister Mary started missing school because of a fever and joint-muscle pain. The doctors at first did not understand what type of infection might be the cause until her blood was analyzed, which showed a low number of white blood and red blood cells. She also showed decreased appetite and nausea, which caused concern and anxiety around the Old Brown Table for several weeks.

Finally, in early July 1941, she was diagnosed with undulant fever or the less-known medical term brucellosis. The question was, how did she contract this disease. When her parents were asked where they procure their milk, the answer was the William Johnson farm just down the road. The family had been buying the milk from the farm for several years since they no longer had their cow. You would visit the farm with a covered milk pail and get fresh raw milk from the milk house that had just been milked that day. The farm sold most of their milk to the Elm Dairy on East Main Road in Le Roy.

The milk became the immediate suspect, and when it was tested, it showed the presence of Brucella bacteria derived from a sick cow. The primary method of preventing brucellosis is by using good hygiene in producing raw milk products or by pasteurizing all milk that is to be ingested by human beings. That is the main reason all milk purchased today in the market is marked pasteurized. Unfortunately, pasteurization takes out many beneficial qualities in the milk, but it does prevent disease. Mary's parents immediately stopped purchasing milk from the Johnson farm and instead had milk delivered by the Elm Dairy in Le Roy. In the 1940s, milk was still being delivered to the home by a milk truck.

Mary Brown with Pal

Unfortunately, there was no treatment available for undulant fever in 1941. The term antibiotic was first used in 1942 that described any substance that is antagonistic to the growth of other microorganisms. World War Two saw its first use in the military but was not available to the public until after 1945. Fortunately, Mary was able to overcome the disease within a year without the use of any medications. But the Old Brown Table never saw raw milk again.

Wikipedia: Antibiotic, Brucellosis.

What Is That Scar, Frank?

Frank W. Brown, the son of Jack & Nellie Brown, was drafted into the army on May 15, 1941. After basic training at Camp Croft, SC, he was assigned to the 12th Infantry, First Battalion, Company C. On September 8, Frank completed 12 weeks of basic training and was then transferred to specialized training to Ft. Devens,

MA. He was trained in Walkie Talkie communications and then sent to Ft. Dix, NJ, and Ft. Benning, GA, for combat training.

On December 21, 1941, Frank was assigned to Camp Gordon, GA, just outside of Augusta, GA. Here he spent the next two years receiving training and also training recruits to achieve full operational strength for the Regiment. Within one year, he reached the rank of Sergeant and was recognized as a disciplined leader in his unit. Several times he was ordered to serve on Military Police (MP) duty, usually at the canteen or the exchange store.

On Sunday, June 21, 1942, Frank assisting as an MP had to stop three fights between men who had too much beer. The incident resulted in one of the soldiers to develop a grudge against Frank. In the evening, when Frank was returning to his barracks, the soldier hid behind the door. When Frank entered the barracks, he was struck in the head very close to the temple by the butt of an M-1 rifle. His barrack mates found him unconscious, and he was taken to the hospital for treatment. The blow could have been fatal since it was so close to the temple, the skull could have been penetrated. Sgt. Vic Santangelo, Frank's best friend, found out who the culprit was and when he found the soldier alone, he beat the daylights out of him to serve as a lesson to the others. There were two weeks that Frank

Billy & Sgt. Frank W. Brown

was in recovery and did not write a letter home but usually explained his writing gap to being absent for specialized training. He never wanted to cause his parents to worry. However, a few months later, when Frank did get home on furlough, they were sitting at the Old Brown Table when Mom noticed the scar just above and to the side of his eyebrow. Frank, of course, minimized the injury, but Dad and Mom realized that it could have been fatal. Frank received notice that he should keep his parents informed on all happenings, both good and bad, but 15 months later, this was challenged by another close call.

The Fourth Division was sent to Camp Gordon Johnston in the Florida panhandle on September 25, 1943, for amphibious training since high-level plans were now in the making for the invasion of Northern Europe. The invasion would be an amphibious assault of the largest scale in human history. The primary assault boat was called the Higgins boat, which was designed to be lightweight, hold about 25 troops, and be capable of landing troops close to shore in shallow waters. Camp Gordon Johnston was an ideal place for the practice of ship to shore landings since its Gulf of Mexico beaches were close in terrain to the beaches in Northern Europe. It was during this training that Sgt. Frank Brown had a very close call to death. On the weapons range, he was instructing a recruit on the use of grenades. When the soldier went to throw the grenade, he pulled the pin as trained, but in the process of giving it a good arm throw, he panicked and dropped it right in front of them. Frank grabbed the soldier and pulled him behind a barrier just a moment before the grenade exploded, throwing shrapnel everywhere.

Well, Frank did not tell his parents again, but the truth did come out when they found out from one of his buddies. The Old Brown Table heard the call of fear and anxiety once again, and his parents thought maybe it was better if they did not know all of the dangers a serviceman faces in the military.

What, Held Back in Seventh?

When I was twelve years old, I was in the seventh grade at District #11 in Jug City, New York. I'm not sure why it was named Jug City because there were only a few houses, and its central feature was the one-room schoolhouse and the O-At-Ka creek. The schoolhouse was one mile from the Brown homestead, which required me to walk to school every day through snow, wind, rain, or sunshine. I have fond memories of that one-room schoolhouse except toward the end, which I will explain later. I entered first grade on September 8, 1941. For those of you who are younger, a one-room schoolhouse usually had only one teacher that taught all eight grammar school grades. Can you believe that? If there were over twenty children, then the teacher would have an aide, but at District #11, there were only about a dozen children at different grade levels in the early forties.

I enjoyed my time at the school from September to June since there were so many things I liked to do, especially during the morning, noon, and afternoon recess. In the winter, we would play in the basement if the weather was nasty and would enjoy playing tag or going through the coal pile to pull out blue foil tags that identified the hard anthracite coal. During the noon one-hour period, we would quickly eat our packed lunch out of our lunch pails so we could go down to the O-At-Ka creek and play a game of hockey on the ice. If we had an assistant teacher, she would escort us, and we would be so involved in the game we would be late for class at 1:00 pm and ketch heck. Our hockey sticks were any kind of tree limb we could find along the bank, and the puck was a piece of driftwood. Who needs pricy equipment to have a good time?

District #11 in Jug City

In the summer, we would play outside a game of kick the can or sandlot baseball, and the recess would pass quickly. Of course, there were the usual difficult times, like when an older boy held a snake over my head or ate my lunch and bullied me. Then the time I was bitten by a local dog that put teeth marks on my hand. That did call for a response from my Dad. How could I forget playing down by the creek where there was a barn with a hayloft and a long rope you could swing on from the loft. How we never fell and break a bone, I do not know. Indeed, the guardian angels were watching over us.

In the fifth grade, the number of students dwindled to around seven, five girls and two boys. The teacher would give you an assignment from your arithmetic, English, science, or health book, which you would study to prepare for being called on. At some point, you would then be called upfront to the teacher's desk to answer questions. One time I was contacted about my science assignment to answer a question on how long it would take to circumnavigate the globe. I answered 90 minutes, which was met with laughter by everyone that heard, including the teacher. "What a ridiculous answer, nothing can move that fast. You are reading too many Flash Gordon books", she exclaimed. It was correct that I was reading Flash Gordon books from our mini library and was always fascinated by Flash's telescope and how he could see people on the moon. Well, the laugh is on them today in what we now know. Space Station orbits the earth every 95 minutes, so I was only 5 minutes off. Also, it is ironic I ended up working for NASA for 32 years.

When I entered seventh grade, we had six in the class, four girls and two boys. The other boy was a year older than me by the name of Bill Dooley. The teacher spent most of the time on one student whom she was preparing at the eighth-grade level to enter high school next year. She spent very little time with me, and I became very bored to the point where I would fool around with Bill Dooley, who was quite a mischief-maker. We were scolded many times, and when December came, the teacher sent a note home that she was going to hold me back since I was not progressing at the seventh-grade level. A conference was arranged with my parents, who naturally were quite upset about me repeating the seventh grade. You can be assured my parents held a conversation around the Old Brown Table that evening, and the decision was made to transfer me to the Grade School in Le Roy. Now, this was before there were buses, so my Dad had to leave me off in the morning and pick me up after work.

Billy & Girlfriends at District #11

In retrospect, my parents made a wise decision. Even though the transition to the Grade School was a very difficult one, the teachers were very understanding and helped me through the transition. Good-by District #11, Miss. Rudolph and your class of six. Within a year, a referendum was passed to centralize the Le Roy school district, and all of the country schools were closed.

Where Are the Statues of the Saints?

Growing up in a Roman Catholic family, we faithfully attended 7:30 am church services every Sunday at Saint Joseph's'. There were two Catholic churches in Le Roy, Saint Josephs, and Saint Peters. Those who attended Saint Josephs were primarily of Italian descent, whereas Saint Peters carried all other nationalities.

In 1941 a new priest was assigned to St Joseph's by the name of Father Ormsby, who was also of Italian descent. He was a young priest, very efficient, quick, and very direct in speech, who led all members to know that he was in charge and would not take any criticism from anyone. Usually, the service called the Mass takes about one hour, but Father Ormsby could perform the service in about 45 minutes, which would delight the parishioners. He soon informed the members that the church building needed an upgrade inside and out, and an increase in tithing was necessary. Now that did not go over very well. Then the old altar was removed, and a more modern one was installed with a majesty crown placed on the ceiling above, giving the appearance of a king's royal throne. Recessed lights were installed over the entire ceiling giving a brilliance throughout the auditorium. Then a side confessional was provided on the right side of the auditorium with a red and green light to inform you if the confessional was occupied or not. These changes were generally welcomed by the members except some of the elderly

Saint Josephs on Lake Street

Italians who did not accept any change, especially when it costs money.

The front of the auditorium, beside the altar and along the right and left side hung many life-size statues of the saints. Many of these statues were gifts of the members over the years. As a young child, I would sometimes stare at these statues with the dim lights of the auditorium and experience a scary sensation, feeling the saints were staring at me. Then one Sunday morning, a change occurred, which was almost unforgivable. When the members entered the auditorium that fateful Sunday, they were met with a new appearance. All of the statues were gone! When it came time for the sermon, Father Ormsby informed the members that the statues were a safety hazard to the members since many of them weighing 200 to 300 pounds were hanging by only one nail. Then he stated the unimaginable, "All of these old statues precariously hanging by a nail I had removed and taken to the Le Roy dump. Anyone of these statues could have fallen and killed someone!" The members were shocked beyond belief that such an act had been committed.

Now the Old Brown Table heard quite a discussion that evening with a general agreement with Father Ormsby's actions. They say that time heals and after all, they all knew who was in control at St Josephs', Father Ormsby, of course!

Who Left the Car Door Open?

It was a typical upstate New York cold winter night when we returned home after visiting relatives in Dad's 1936 Chevy. In those days, cars usually did not come with heaters, so Dad had installed one under the dash on the front passenger side. Unfortunately, the heater did not provide sufficient heat for the back seat, so we always had a blanket to place on our lap and legs to keep warm. We were incredibly thankful for that luxury as simple as it was.

Mom had seven sisters that lived locally in the Le Roy area, so it was the usual practice, especially on the weekend, to visit my aunts for an evening of playing cards, celebrating a birthday, or just getting together for a social visit. Now I just loved these social gatherings because there was always a lot of laughter and some good eating as well. Toward the end of the evening, my aunts would put on a snack that was more like a dinner, and the little ones would partake until our bellies would almost bust.

Now the only drawback of these joyous visits was returning home late, which for an eight-year-old would be around 11 pm. On one of these occasions upon returning home very sleepy-eyed, I got out of the back seat of the 1936 Chevy sedan, and more than likely left the rear car door open. Now the 1936 Chevy front doors opened like car doors do today that is they are hinged toward the front of the vehicle. At that time, the rear doors were hinged toward the rear, which is the opposite of today's vehicles. As a result of this design, they were called suicide doors because if you opened them, they would catch anything if the car was moving forward.

Billy & 1936 Chevy

Well, that late dark, cold winter evening, we exited the car by the farmhouse back door, which was our usual routine before Dad would move the car into the barn, about 200 feet from the farmhouse. That late evening Dad must have been tired as well since he moved quickly into the barn and was stunned by a loud crashing sound that we could hear in the farmhouse. It was only a few minutes later when the Old Brown Table overheard an irate father informing all of us that someone had left the rear car door open on the right side of the vehicle and when he entered the barn the car door struck the side of the barn and it was bent completely back! Everyone except I was looking at each other, trying to remember who had committed this destructive act. Naturally, all eyes turned to me since I was the baby of the family and would typically take the blame. I don't remember if there were any consequences for such a careless act except the Old Brown Table would know if it could only talk.

Now, Dad was not one to take his pride and joy 36 Chevy to a repair shop. Dad went to work and somehow put the door back in position on the body, BUT we could no longer use that door for fear that it may fall off. One day somebody did use the door, and we all gasped with the fear that we would find the door on the ground. The door held, so we were all relieved as witnessed by the Old Brown Table.

Now that was a constant reminder to me for the next three years until Dad bought a new 1949 Chevy with only two front doors. He told us at the Old Brown Table that it was fewer doors to whistle and be knocked off. Now, who could argue with that analysis!

LRGN: 1-20-1949.

Who Rang the Dinner Bell?

The Dinner Bell restaurant owned by Mrs. Olive Nichols was considered one of the finest restaurants in Le Roy with modest prices and delicious food. After being open for four years, it was destroyed by fire on December 26, 1949. Upon rebuilding, it was reopened on Monday, April 17, 1950, with many improvements in the kitchen and dining area. However, before the fire late in 1949, the Dinner Bell encountered a rather bizarre accident.

Now before I continue with the story as witnessed by the Old Brown Table, I need to introduce you to one of my relatives by the name of John Docking, who lived on South Street in Le Roy. John was married to my cousin Johanna Longhini, the daughter of Nicholas and Johanna Longhini. The best way to describe John was flamboyant, outgoing, daring, outspoken, and I must say it, "a little crazy." I, a teenager, well-liked John because he was so entertaining and always put on a show. As a child, when visiting his home on South Street, we would talk about the two Egyptian mummies he had stored upstairs at his house. John had a rich uncle that traveled worldwide and one time brought home two Egyptian mummies, which ended up in Docking's home. I was able to view these mummies when they were displayed by Docking at a local carnival sideshow, which required an admission ticket.

So now that you know about Docking, we will get on with the time when John rang the dinner bell. On July 11, 1949, John was enjoying himself at Callan's saloon on Bank Street. After several drinks, he was bragging that he could ride a motorcycle. To demonstrate, John walked into the alley between Callan's bar and O'Geen's shoe repair shop, hopped on a parked motorcycle, and came roaring out of the alley entirely out of control. He and the cycle shot across Bank Street, dashed up a small incline next to the sidewalk, cleared two stone steps, and crashed through double wooden doors of the Dinner Bell kitchen. The kitchen was usually a beehive of activity at the eatery but was fortunately vacant since the restaurant was closed for the day. Just by chance, the doors were in the path because on either side was a brick wall of the building. Not so, forgiving!

Docking picked himself up from underneath the rubble, which covered the cycle and walked away from the accident. He was later treated for cuts and bruises at the local doctor's office and then taken to Police Justice Arthur H. Holthaus and fined $25 for reckless driving. Estimates of damage to the restaurant were around $1800, which included a steam table, a large number of dishes, the door, and the doorframe. The motorcycle, which was parked at the rear of the A & P store by the assistant manager, Herbert McCalfery, ended up with a sprung frame.

The same day early in the morning, a red-faced Le Roy police officer was trying to explain how his police car rolled down the creek bank by the Moose Lodge and was partially dipped in O-At-Ka Creek. The officer escaped a dunking but not an admonishment by the Chief.

Now that is not the end of the story about John Docking. He continued to live a hazardous lifestyle. In the late '50s, his rich uncle gave him a four-door Chrysler, which he immediately rolled over to destruction. Somehow John ended up in Batavia and ran the Docking Motel on the Westside. I wonder if there is where he kept the Egyptian mummies. Sound familiar to the Bates Motel in the movie Psycho?

LRGN: 7-14-49; 4-13-1950.

Woman's Scream on A Cold Winter Night

On a cold winter night, March 5, 1942, the Brown family was seated in the living room listening to the evening radio programs. The radio was a nightly occurrence since excellent programs were broadcast over the local stations. Around 10:30 pm there was a horrible scream heard through the cold crisp air that did not seem to stop. It was a woman's scream that announced fear, horror and fright. My Dad and brother Al put on their winter coats and went outside to determine the source of the scream. A woman met them on the road, just a few hundred feet from the house. She was yelling and screaming that a car hit her husband and a friend. Jim Burrows, who lived at the corner of Cole and Warsaw Road, checked the older injured man and could not detect a pulse. A younger man was lying in the ditch in a snowbank and was severely injured. There was no car in sight indicating the driver of the vehicle that hit the pedestrians had runoff. My Dad ran to Mrs. Meehan at the corner and telephoned the Le Roy police department to call an ambulance to the scene.

The following is an account taken from the Le Roy Gazette News, March 11, 1942, which headlined on the front page, "Charge Grows Out of Fatal Accident, Le Royan Fled After Car Struck Pedestrian." The article went on to say, Samuel Brown, died of a fractured skull. Stanley Davis faces criminal negligence charge. Remanded Saturday from the Genesee County jail on $500 bail, Stanley D Davis, 36, of the Le Roy-Pavilion road is awaiting a hearing before Justice of the Peace Clarence B. Crocker on a charge of criminal negligence on Tuesday afternoon, March 10.

Davis was alleged to have fled in his automobile after striking down and fatally injuring Samuel Brown, 24-years-old, as he was walking along the Le Roy-Pavilion road about two miles south of the village at 10:30 pm Thursday. Suffering a fractured skull, Brown died at 10:15 am the next day at St. Jerome Hospital in Batavia without regaining consciousness.

According to Police Captain Fred J. Rider, Samuel Brown, his wife, Clara, 22, and Clyde Edward Lane, Jr., 13, were returning from spending the evening at the home of James Burrell, just 50 yards distant. They were walking south on the east side of the road facing traffic when the accident occurred.

Mrs. Brown jumped to the center of the road out of range when the car approached from the rear. Her husband was thrown up onto the hood and then jostled off the back of the vehicle. The Lane boy was hit by the right fender and hurled into a snowbank, escaping with lacerations and body bruises.

Police Captain Rider was continuing the investigation of the accident about 1:45 am Friday when he noticed a car in the Davis driveway. Inspecting the machine, he discovered the radiator grill was bent, and the radiator hood dented. Davis had not yet retired and was taken by the officer to Le Roy Police Headquarters, where after being questioned, he admitted being the driver of the machine that struck Brown.

Brown was a native of Rappahannock, VA, and observed his 24th birthday last June 25. He had worked on farms in the area for the past seven years and was an employee on a farm operated by Clyde Edward Lane, Sr., and owned by Dr. W. D. Johnson of Batavia. The Old Brown Table witnessed a dreadful tragedy that cold winter night in March 1942 that the family would not forget for years to come.

LRGN: 3-5-1942.

You Bought a Hoover?

It was mid-1941, and the United States was just starting to pull out of the Great Depression. Money was tight, inflation high at 9%, and wages low, so purchasing something for the home took some thought and was usually questioned by the phrase, "Do we need this?" Buying a new car was out of the question, so used cars were in demand. The country was gearing up the war machine since Hitler had already invaded Poland in 1939, and it only seemed a matter of time, and we would be at war. Just a few months later, on December 7, 1941, Pearl Harbor occurred, and our country declared war on Japan and Germany within a few days.

In May 1941, Mom and Dad purchased a Philco tabletop radio for the amount of $35 ($615 in $2020), which seems very high by our standards today. Remember, television was only a recent invention, and there were practically no broadcast stations. In fact, on July 1, 1941, the first commercial station was begun.

One day a salesman came to our door, which was common in those days, and demonstrated the Hoover vacuum cleaner at the Old Brown Table. He was from the Economy store in Le Roy and put on a good show on why my Mom needed a vacuum cleaner, which she never had. It was common practice to take the rugs outside in the summer and beat them with wire beaters to take out the dirt and dust. Routine cleaning was done with a hand pushed brush sweeper.

Well, Mom fell in love with the Hoover and decided to buy it at the cost of $49 ($860 in $2020) without Dad's knowledge since he was at work at the time. Dinner was put on the table as was the custom at 5:00 pm, and the six of us started to eat dinner. That is when Mom broke the news to Dad, and it was met with immediate opposition. Dad said we could not afford it, and he got up from the table, took the Hoover, and immediately returned it to the Economy store in town. We were all stunned when Mom burst into tears, got up from the table, and ran into the bedroom. We just sat there with not much of an appetite since we very seldom witnessed Mom and Dad argue or disagree.

A few months later, Mom had her Hoover. Wives can be quite persuasive, as all of us married folks and the Old Brown Table know.

You're Going to Shoot Your Eye Out Kid!

Like any young boy, I, at the age of twelve, wanted a BB gun, and I'm sure my parents were anxious in satisfying such a request. But Dad being a good father, saw this as a growing point in a young boy's life, and over the objections of my Mom, I received a Daisy air rifle in the summer of 1947. Over the next few weeks, I enjoyed using my newly acquired gift shooting at tin cans, glass jars, cardboard targets, and once a bird, which I immediately regretted killing and vowed no more live animal targets. Also, no more glass jars since picking up the pieces took too long, and I was at risk of cutting my fingers. I foolishly demonstrated this when I placed a gallon jug on a stand and blasted it to pieces. Upon picking up the pieces, one large piece of glass fell and hit my left forearm, putting a deep cut into my flesh with a resultant gush of blood. A quick run to the farmhouse for first aide convinced me that was enough glass targets.

What took the cake, however, was when four boys from down the road brought over their BB guns, of course to show off their new hardware. Each of us thought we had the best weapon, and we bragged how good a shot we were. Now I must admit we were not practicing proper gun safety as we pointed our Red Ryder and Daisy air rifles in the air and fired off a round or two. During this reckless show-off demonstration, I lowered my rifle and accidentally fired a round into the face of one of my friends. He yelled in astonishment that I had shot him, and he pointed to his face where there was a small dimple the size of a BB just one inch below his eye. That scared all of us and me that I could have taken my friend's eyesight with one fast careless act. That incident taught me, and I hope my boyhood friends that safety is number one when using any type of weapon. The Old Brown Table did not hear this reckless act that evening since I knew if my parents listened to this tale, the BB gun would be gone forever.

A few years later, I was allowed to fire my Dad's 22 caliber rifle, and I was now convinced more than ever to practice gun safety. With that said, my Dad permitted me to use the gun to kill woodchucks in the field and rats that were in our barn and eating the chicken feed in the attached chicken coop. So, I would sit on the back steps of the farmhouse and, with a good view of the open door of the chicken coop, look for rats eating the feed. It wasn't long before I saw a rat in the feed trough, but I could not get a fair shot. Soon the rat moved to the water bucket for a drink, and I took aim through the scope and fired off a round entering right through the back of the rat, dropping him into the pail of water. Wow, this was great fun, so after disposing of the rat, I took my place on the back steps and waited to see if another rat would follow the same routine. Soon another appeared more remarkable than the first one eating the feed. This time he did not take long before he needed a drink from the pail, and as he leaned over the bucket for a drink, I took aim through the scope and took the shot. This time I missed the rat, but to my horror hit the pail. The rat with an extension on his life ran off, and I approached the chicken coop with caution only to observe I had shot a big hole in the side of the pail. I was using a hollow point 22 caliber round, which, upon impact, creates a large hole. Now at the Old Brown Table, I had to inform my Dad that he needed to buy a new pail for the chicken coop. He took it well but advised me to take a better aim in the future.

We always felt safe on the small farm just two miles south of Le Roy until one day, an incident occurred that shook our confidence. The Baltimore & Ohio railroad tracks boarded our property on the west side. Several times a day and night, you would hear a freight train and occasionally a passenger train. Along one side of the single track were high voltage electric lines with large insulators that sometimes were the targets for an irresponsible sharpshooter. We could hear these shots now and then and did not know if they were shooting at rabbits or the insulators. One day while in the back yard of the old farmhouse, I heard a rifle shot and a high-pitched whistle pass overhead. My Dad was outside with me, and we both screamed toward the tracks to stop the target practice. They yelled back, and that, fortunately, ended the incident. So much for the back yard safe zone!

> "He will cover you with his pinions,
> And under his wings you will find refuge;
> His faithfulness is a shield and buckler."
> Psalm 91:4

Chapter Five

1950 To 1960 Old Brown Table Tales

A Girl Named Barbara

In the late 1940s, a family by the name of Burdick moved into the old brown shingled house just one-quarter mile south of the Old Brown Table on Warsaw Road. They were a farm family renting the home from Dr. W. A. Johnson to work on the dairy farm across the road. There were three boys and one girl named Barbara, who used a wheelchair since she had contracted infantile paralysis commonly called polio. The late '40s and early '50s experienced a dramatic increase in polio across the country. The Old Brown Table heard many conversations expressing fear that this demon disease could strike anyone at any time, child or adult, and now it was hitting very close to home. The worst part was the cause was unknown, so how could one take measures to prevent contracting this disease.

Barbara Burdick

Almost overnight, the person experiences muscle weakness resulting in the inability to move. The liability often involves the legs but can also affect the muscles of the head, neck, and diaphragm. In those with muscle weakness, about 2 to 5% of children and 15 to 30% of adults die. Unfortunately, this was the case for Barbara.

Barbara was a lovely girl with a pleasant, joyful disposition despite the disease that had struck her at such an early age. Her brothers would push her down the road to our house in her wheelchair so she could play cards with me or listen to my accordion music. She loved to ask me if I would play 52 Pickup, and when I said yes, she would throw the cards in the air and, with a hardy laugh, say, "Pick them up!" In the winter of 1951, Barbara contracted pneumonia, and with her weak lungs, she succumbed to the disease peacefully passing away at home. The wake was held in their farm-house, and her parents asked if I would take a picture of Barbara in her coffin since they did not have a camera.

During this period of the early '50s, progress was being made on a polio vaccine. In the USA, Dr. Jonas Salk at the University of Pittsburgh announced the success of a polio vaccine on April 12, 1955, which was highly successful after three doses providing 99% immunity. Unfortunately, this was too late for Barbara. Still, life went on, and a few years later, the Burdick family moved across the street until, eventually, they moved to another farming location. Looking back, Barbara taught me as well as many others that life can be filled with joy regardless of your situation in life, whether it be your health or status.

Billy, You Are All White!

To help pay for my college expenses to attend the Engineering School at the University of Buffalo, I worked regular labor jobs during my summer breaks from June through August. My first job was at the Lapp Insulator factory, which was only two miles from the old farmhouse. I would be dropped off by my Dad for the 7 AM to 4 PM shift. It was challenging to get a summer job since the Le Roy factories primarily wanted to fill full-time yearly positions. I was fortunate since my Dad had relatives working at the plant who put in a word for me, and I was able to secure a 40-hour per week job in Bob Smith's insulator turning department.

The Lapp factory manufactured ceramic insulators for the electric power industry and shipped their product worldwide. The department that I worked in would take various sized ingots of dried clay and turn them on a lathe to circular clay forms, which then would be glazed and fired in a high-temperature oven to bring the clay to a sturdy ceramic state. The electric power companies would then place the insulators on power distribution poles and attach wires for transmission of electric power.

Since the turning department would cut the clay on a lathe, a considerable amount of white dust was generated, and powerful blowers would remove about 90 percent with the remaining gathering on workman's clothes and the surrounding environment. On returning home after the first day, the Old Brown Table heard Mom exclaim, "Billy, you are white from head to toe. Get those dirty clothes off, and into the washer, they will go!" I would wash up before supper, and Mom would place my clothes in the washer at least every other day. I worked at Lapp for two consecutive summers and became used to the white dust. Sometimes I wonder how much I gathered in my lungs, which could not be washed out.

In my Junior college year, I got a chance through my brother to get a job at a Canada Dry bottling plant on Mt. Read Boulevard in Rochester, New York, about 25 miles from Le Roy. It paid very well at $1.75 per hour and was without the perpetual white dust. The only drawback was the 25-mile commute five days per week and working the second shift from 4 to 12 PM. Dad would come home from work, and I would use his 1949 Chevy for the commute. I was assigned to a four-person crew at the bottling plant who would remove the empty bottles from the distribution trucks and then fill the trucks with full bottles for the next day delivery. One benefit I unconsciously received was building up my arm and back muscles due to the lifting of crates of bottles. Yes, that is correct glass bottles, since, in the mid-fifties, plastic and metal cans had not yet come into existence.

One night we had the unusual task of breaking up 400 five-gallon jugs of the root beer syrup into a 55-gallon barrel with holes in the bottom to drain out the smelly sticky syrup. We had a great time that night, and as an added benefit, we could take some of the 5-gallon jugs home for our personal use. Mom never had so much root beer syrup to use for whatever purpose, but I do know we had a lot of root beer floats.

One evening after a month on the job, we were short one man, so the foreman trained me on how to use a forklift so pallets could be moved into the loading area for movement of glass bottled pop. The training amounted to the use of the pedals and control lever for moving the two front forks into pallets and lifting the pallets for placement of the load. I liked the responsibility the foreman was placing in my hands. Upon his orders, I moved the forklift to retrieve some pallets. The forklift responded readily to my every command as I spotted a large stack of pallets probably 30 feet high. I moved the two-pronged fork upward then forward into a pile of eight pallets. Next, I lifted the pallets upward, which turned out to be a fatal mistake. Unknowingly a few pallets had attached to a rear stack of pallets, and as I lifted upward, a rear stack lifted a well, so when I pulled the forklift back, the rear stack of pallets rotated forward toward me. All I remember was seeing a tall stack of pallets coming directly toward me and the forklift. With cunning instincts, using all my strength, I leaped from the forklift just in time as four or five pallets hit the machine with a loud crash.

I picked myself off the floor and just stood there in horror. The foreman came running around the corner, and with astonishment showing in his haggard face shouted, are you hurt. I was glad he was concerned about my welfare, but his real concern was about the damaged forklift and his embarrassment in providing me with such a short and inadequate training. I watched as he straightened out the rear metal battery cover and the misaligned forklift finger controls. He told me abruptly to go back to loading-trucks, and he would take care of the forklift. The repairs were quickly made, and he soon had the forklift in operation, but I was never asked to operate the truck again.

The next morning, however, the Old Brown Table heard of my harrowing event accompanied by a frightened stare from my Mom and Dad. I think they preferred white clay dust to Canada Dry!

Blow Out

What is it about home cooking that brings up fond memories? My Mom was a fantastic cook that I did not fully appreciate until I became an adult and left home for service in the Air Force. The Old Brown Table witnessed many delicious meals for over 90 years in the farmhouse kitchen. Mom would always scour the newspaper for new recipes, which she would give a try without fear of failure.

Now being an Italian family, you would think we would eat spaghetti or pasta every day of the week. Not true! The only day we had spaghetti on a routine basis was for Sunday noon dinner. Mom would make her spaghetti sauce from tomatoes grown in the garden every year. She was an avid canner, including tomatoes, tomato sauce, and catsup, along with fruits such as applesauce, pears, cherries, and peaches. Since we had a grape vineyard, she would bottle grape juice and make grape jelly. Another favorite was canned creamed corn, which made delicious corn chowder. Then there was strawberry, blueberry, and quince jam.

Mom Preparing Dinner

One day Mom purchased a new appliance called a pressure cooker, which was the rage at the time since it could cook a meal so fast. She loved her pressure cooker and prepared many a meal with it. I do remember one day, though, when things went incredibly wrong. It was the day when the Old Brown Table was shaken to its core. Mom had placed a chicken in the pressure cooker and put it on the electric burner to generate steam inside the vessel. A small metal bobber at the top of the cooker would bounce back and forth as a method of ventilating steam so it would not reach high pressure and ultimately explode. Turning the lid locked it to the top of the cooker.

I was upstairs in my bedroom above the kitchen when I heard a loud explosion. I was startled and ran downstairs as fast as I could when I met Mom in the kitchen with a frightened expression on her face. The pressure cooker had reached a pressure high enough where it blew the rubber relief valve out of the cooker lid. There was a lot of steam pouring out when she carefully pulled it off the burner. Above the pressure cooker and stove, displayed on the ceiling, were a lot of fragmented chicken pieces. We found out later after viewing the situation that the chicken was too large for the pressure cooker, and it had blocked the vent in the lid where the steam passes through the bobber. Steam pressure kept building up until it blew out the rubber relief valve.

Well, that was the end of pressure-cooking for my Mom. I never saw one in the kitchen again. The Old Brown Table was relieved as well!

Darlyn, What is Wrong?

In 1956 my Dad and Mom (Manny & Eleanor Costa) lived next door to my Grandpa and Grandma Brown on Warsaw Road. One great thing about living next door was that we had dinner at Grandmas many a Sunday. I, Darlyn, would often visit early and help by peeling potatoes, setting the table, and help wherever I could. Grandma was an excellent cook. Roast pork, fried chicken, roast beef, or turkey all of which was delicious. Afterward, we sat around the Old Brown Table and discussed various subjects usually with coffee and pie. Over holidays there was always additional family and I'm not sure how we all fit around that Old Brown Table. We all helped clean up with more conversation and laughter and Grandma was by this time exhausted and ready for a long afternoon nap.

Grandma loved to can various homegrown fruit but one, in particular, was indeed quite strange. Have you ever heard of quinces? They grew on two trees behind the old farmhouse. They smelled like pineapple in the late fall, when they were ready to be picked. Grandma made delicious quince jelly and a few years ago my daughter Sherry ordered some from Amazon, which was not nearly as good as

Grandmas. Now I have a quince tree and make my quince jelly but somehow it is never as good as the memory of hers.

When I was about seven years old living in the "little house," my Mom was pregnant with Marilyn. One day Mom decided to make cookies even though she was tired, and it was a warm day. I was playing on the living room floor when I heard her scream yelling frantically to call Grandpa! She somehow caught her pinky finger in the electric mixer. I had never been taught to use the phone, so I froze. Mom then told me to run next door and get Grandpa. My legs ran as fast as I could, opened the door to Grandpa's house, and found Grandpa and Grandma talking at the Old Brown Table. Since I was taught not to interrupt, I hesitated, but when they saw the frightened expression on my face, they immediately asked what was wrong. I told them the plight my Mom was in, and Grandpa immediately grabbed some tools, and they all ran back to the "little house." The mixer was stilled turned on, so he immediately turned it off, and using pliers bent the mixer blades so Mom could remove her hand. In the meantime, Grandma called the doctor. The doctor came to the house, bandaged her finger, and drove her to the hospital in Batavia. Yes, doctors made house calls still in the 1950s and even provided transportation to the hospital.

The Old Brown Table later that day heard the report that the finger was not broken, only a severe laceration. Soon after that, I learned to use the phone.

Ref: Darlyn (Costa) Hawkins.

Don't Drink the Water

$\mathcal{A}t$ the old homestead, when you wanted a drink of cold water, you would go to the kitchen sink near the Old Brown Table, and take water from the sink faucet to satisfy your thirst. The bathroom also had water, but you did not drink water from there because it was set up with rainwater from the cistern. We collected rainwater from the roof gutters, which fed the cistern. The rainwater was very soft water used for taking a bath or washing clothes but not for drinking since I was told there could be a dead mouse in the cistern. Was that a possibility or just a scare tactic?

The water in the kitchen was termed hard water taken from a well 25 feet from the house. It was technically termed sulfur water since it had a strong odor of hydrogen sulfide. In other words, it stunk to high heaven. When you are brought up drinking sulfur water, you don't know any difference, so what did it matter. I couldn't understand the terrible look on our guest's face when they tasted the water and asked what was in it. Then they wanted to drink the rain (cistern) water, which was a no-no, so we offered them a soda.

When I entered military service and would come home on leave, I found out that I could not drink the water either. How did I ever accept the stinky water during my childhood? Even when you made orange juice you could detect the strong odor of sulfur. Since the water had a high mineral content, it was classified hard and in time would line the water pipes with an orange substance. My Mom had an old country teakettle for heating water for coffee, tea, or general cooking. It, too, was encrusted with this strange orange substance, and she would break it out with a chisel and hammer every so often. Sometimes this would cause a leak in the teakettle. Did she throw it away and then buy a new one? Heavens NO! All she would do is take some cold tap water, boil it in the teakettle, and the strange orange material would soon seal it up.

I have often wondered what that sulfur water did to our insides after drinking it for several years. Maybe the Old Brown Table knows?

Fire Fire!

Easter vacation was always a welcome relief from school, and it came during the beautiful springtime of the year. In a good year, the temperature would warm to the 50s and sometimes climb to the 60s, which is welcome in upper New York State after a cold, snowy hard winter. Now spring is usually the winter cleanup time of the year so that Billy would get the rake and, with the sun shining brightly, would pick up leaves and small limbs blown down out of the trees.

Now he had seen his Dad burn field grass and leaves near the house, so he started a fire in a small area near the garden. He had a steel flat shovel used in mixing sand and cement, which was handy for smothering the fire to control the burn area.

It was a bright sunny morning and provided such an uplifting feeling compared to the confinement of the school classroom. It was going quite well when all of a sudden, a wind blew up, and the fire started spreading fast. Billy tried to keep up controlling the path of the fire, but it was becoming almost impossible. Then when he would frantically stamp the fire with the flat side of the shovel, it would send up sparks, which the wind would carry to more dry grass. The smoke was becoming intense gagging Billy, and his face was burning from the heat.

Suddenly Billy heard his sister Eleanor calling, "Billy, are you okay?" I yelled frantically, "I can no longer control the fire!" Eleanor ran in the house, and unknown to me called the Le Roy Fire Department. The grass fire with the wind picking up took off toward the barn, and the flames licked the concrete foundation. Billy thought the barn is going to catch fire, and there is nothing I can do to stop it. Fortunately, the barn had a two-foot-high concrete foundation, which shielded the wood siding from the flames. The fire now roaring out of control swept around the barn and turned north toward Le Roy. If it had turned south, it would have engulfed the 2000 Norway spruce trees, which had been just planted the prior year.

Billy barely heard the fire trucks blaring sirens approaching the homestead on Pavilion road, and when he looked up, he saw several men in fire gear walking fast-paced through the field from the roadway. Billy slowly walked up toward the front of the barn where his Dad, who had been called from work, met him. His Dad never made a critical remark or scolded him to his surprise. Billy was just too exhausted and could only remark he regretted starting the fire. We were very fortunate that the fire did not burn through the grape vineyard as it moved to the forest edge of the Charlie Robert's property. However, the Old Brown Table heard that evening, the hazard of starting a fire alone, especially without first consulting Dad.

When Billy looked down at his watch to see the time, he was surprised to see that the watch works had separated from the watch metal case caused by pounding the ground hard with the shovel to extinguish the flames. This was his prize Superman watch, which his sister Mary had given him at Christmas. Thank the Lord this was the only casualty of the fire.

Grapes, Grapes, Grapes

Sometime in the mid-1920s, Charles and Jack Brown planted around three acres of Concord grapes to the north of the homestead. It took about three years before the grapes were producing enough where they could be harvested and sold at markets in town or front of the homestead on Warsaw Road. Grapes are a very hardy fruit to grow, but they take a considerable amount of hard work. In the Spring, the vines have to be pruned back and tied to the support wire, or you will not produce any fruit in six months. Then throughout the summer, the weeds have to be kept down and the vines cultivated. When mid-September arrives, it is time to harvest the grapes. However, sometimes an early frost would be forecast, and definite steps would be taken to prevent harm to the grapes. The Old Brown Table witnessed the anxiety in a conversation that the grape harvest could be lost. Dad would take old railroad ties and light several fires in the vineyard to just provide enough heat and smoke to shield the grapes from the frost.

Grape Vineyard

There were only a few days to pick the grapes when they were dark purple. Dad would hire relatives to harvest all day on Saturday, and all would be invited to supper to finish the day. Grapes were picked, and bunches placed in bushel containers. Dad had a large wheeled cart that would fit between the rows, and he would fill it up with bushels of sweet-smelling grapes and take it to the barn. The entire ground floor of the barn would be filled with bushels of grapes, which would be swarming and buzzing with bees attracted to the sweet grape juice.

Over the next few days, the grapes would be sorted to A quality for selling to the food markets in town or front of our homestead. The B quality grapes were dumped into a hand grinder and ground into a 6-foot diameter by 8-foot-high vat. Grape juice would separate from the pulp and would be drawn off from the bottom of the vat. The pulp would be shoveled into a press where the remainder of the juice would be squeezed out. All of the grape juice would then be poured into sizeable 75-gallon wood barrels and taken to the homestead basement where it would ferment over the next few months to produce red wine. There were always two or three 75-gallon barrels in the cellar, which always offered wine for visiting guests.

Since I was a young boy during those grape harvest years, I would serve as a water boy to deliver ice-cold water to the workers on warm Saturday afternoons. Later I would climb to the roof of the chicken coop to observe the workers below and eat whatever grapes I could consume. Today when I drink grape juice, those memories come back to those days long ago. I wonder if the Old Brown Table remembers as well?

Hazardous Field

The field across Warsaw Road from the old farmhouse always displayed a beautiful view from our kitchen window, whether it was Spring, Summer, or Autumn season. The field, property of Johnson Farms, was usually planted in field corn for the dairy farm down the road. In the late 1940s, the corn was cut with a tractor-pulled side cutter and then stacked in bundles over the entire field, providing a frightful sight on a full moon night.

When the Burdick family lived across the street during the 1950s, they had goats and a horse. The Burdick boys would saddle the horse and ride it in the Johnson field in early Spring or after the corn was harvested in the Fall. On one occasion, I was asked if I would like to ride the horse called Tom. I had never ridden a horse before, so I gladly accepted. The boys threw on the saddle and walked the horse out to the Johnson field, where I placed my right foot in the stirrup and lifted my body onto the saddle. I was amazed at first on how high the horse stood and the immensity of the animal. I took the rains while Ronny Burdick held the bit on the horse's head. They then told me to yell Giddy Up to get the horse in gear. What they did not tell me was to stop Tom, you yell Whoa and pull back on the reins.

Well, I yelled Giddy Up when Ronny let go of the reins, and to my surprise, Tom immediately went into a gallop across the field. I completely surprised yelled Whoa but, in my excitement, did not pull back on the reins. I continued to shout Whoa, but Tom galloped faster with me, bouncing up and down in the saddle. Then I saw with horror that Tom was heading toward the North fence in Johnson's field, and he would probably jump it with me barely able to hang on and the Burdick boys chasing me in total amazement. So, I took the only defensive action I instinctively knew, which was to remove my feet from the stirrups, let go of the reins and jump into the field. I hit the turf hard and went into a roll with Tom racing on until he reached the fence and came to an abrupt halt. The Burdick boys were yelling and laughing with Ronny getting Tom and bringing him back to where I lay embarrassed as to my weak performance. The only causality beside my tarnished pride was a broken rein where Tom had stepped on it while in his getaway gallop. Ronny's father later that day expressed his dismay on my performance and the damaged harness stating, "Anyone can ride a horse on a farm."

In the Fall of that same year, a farmer showed up in Johnson's field with a new Ford tractor plowing the field in nice neat rows preparing the field for next Spring's seeding with a new crop of corn. When the farmer finished plowing, he attached a drag which would break up the clods of rich brown dirt and smooth the field over. I watched the Ford tractor move up and down the field, and when it drew close, the farmer stopped and asked me if I would like a ride. I, of course, said I would, hopped on and sat on the thin fender as the grey Ford effortlessly pulled the drag lifting a cloud of brown dust. When the farmer came to the end of the field, he would make a complete turn to head back across the field. When we went to the end of the field, he stopped and asked me to take the wheel and drive the Ford back on another sweep of the field. He wanted to take a break and get some water to drink at the farmhouse next to the field. He then cautioned me to make a complete turn in the shape of a circle before making another pass. Otherwise, the drag could get caught up in the rear Ford tractor tires and ride up on the tire, causing damage to the tractor tires and the drag.

With that caution off went the farmer while I put the Ford in gear, let out the clutch, and off down the field I went with a feeling of exhilaration on my first vehicle driving experience. When I got to the end of the field, I completely forgot to make the complete circle turn and turned the wheel abruptly to the left to make the next pass. As I was making the abrupt turn, I then realized although too late that the drag would be caught in the tractor tire. I glanced down and saw the drag come very close to the tire, barely touching it when I straightened the wheel out for the next pass. Traveling down the field with a sigh of relief, I then saw the farmer returning to the field, after which I gladly yielded the Ford back into his control.

That evening dinner at the Old Brown Table, the family heard of my exciting adventure of driving the grey Ford tractor, but I somehow withheld telling them the mistake on my illegal U-Turn!

Home Movie Nights

When we entertained relatives and friends, it was a common occurrence to show home movies by setting up an 8mm Kodak projector by the Old Brown Table and project onto a screen in the living room. Adults and children would enjoy seeing themselves in movie shots or even view some purchased movies.

My brother Frank was the one who introduced the family into taking home movies, which at first were black and white and later in color. Now the hobby of home movies was an expensive one in the late 1930s based on the equipment purchase and the movie film. A Kodak 8mm movie camera would cost around $30 ($300 in $2020) and the projector about $40. If that weren't bad enough, the black and white film would cost $3 for a 50 ft. reel, which would only project for six minutes. Then there was the developing cost ($3 for 50 ft. reel), which was only done by Kodak Processing centers, one in Findlay, Ohio, and one in California.

Frank started making movies in 1937, which was followed by his brother Alfred and sister Mary. In 1942 Alfred worked at Eastman Kodak in Rochester, NY, and bought a new Kodak movie camera for Frank, who was in the Army at the time. Frank would take movies at his military base, such as Camp Jordan, in Augusta, GA, and send them home for the family to view.

The children would love to see the purchased films, such as "Jack and the Bean Stalk," "Abbott & Costello Meet the Mummy," Roy Rogers and Gene Autry. Showing a series of silent 8mm movies would take about 2 hours, followed by my Mom dishing out ice cream topped with peanuts and chocolate syrup around the Old Brown Table. Good times cherished, never forgotten!

Is That Gas I Smell?

The author, in his teenage years, always enjoyed a hike through the fields and woods of the old homestead just two miles south of Le Roy. The walks could be solo or with boyhood friends and usually would pass over the property heading north to the O-At-Ka creek. On one of these hikes during the summer of 1951, we paused at the Atlantic Pipeline valve pit, which was at the north end of the property. We usually would lift the cover of the valve pit and smell the gasoline that was invisibly speeding through the 12-inch steel pipeline. This time, however, we got a big surprise.

Upon lifting the 36-inch diameter steel cover, we saw several small pin-size jets of gas flowing horizontally from just below the large circle hand valve. As young teenage boys, we could hardly contain our excitement as we ran top speed across the field to the old farmhouse to announce our discovery. Mom, with calmness, just said, "Wait until your father comes home and show him your discovery." Time seemed to past eternally slow until Dad arrived home at his usual time of 5:00 PM. He patiently listened to us and said, let's have supper, at the Old Brown Table, of course, and then you can show me your discovery.

After supper true to his word, we journeyed across the field to the valve pit where the odor of gas was powerful. Lifting the valve cover and witnessing the leaking of gasoline from at least three small horizontal jets, he told us he would report the leak to the Atlantic Pipeline officials. Dad immediately notified the pipeline, and they responded it would take them three days to be on-site to make repairs. We were surprised by such a delay and could not help but visualize all of that gasoline going to waste by seeping into our good farm soil. A short discussion followed at the Old Brown Table, leading to the conclusion that we could recover some of the gasoline by a straightforward method of using a large tomato juice can with the lid removed and shingle on a four-foot-long stick. The horizontal jet of gas would hit the shingle and fall into the tomato can held by a string. The gas would then be emptied into a five-gallon gas can, taken to the farmhouse and emptied into a 55-gallon drum used for fueling the doodlebug, Dad's farm tractor.

Dad gave us the responsibility for this recovery effort. I immediately went to the woodshed, made three sticks with a wooden shingle attached, and found three tomato cans, one of which had to be emptied of tomato juice. We then raced to the valve cover, and to our amazement, the method worked very well even though it was relatively slow since it took around 5 minutes to fill one can. The next day we started at daybreak and noticed the horizontal jets were now larger in diameter and flow. It took only 4 minutes and on the third day only 2 minutes.

On the fourth day about mid-day, the Atlantic Pipeline repair crew arrived and, to our surprise, were accompanied by six 8000-gallon tanker trucks. My friend and I watched with an intent curiosity as the back-hoe dug a large pit around the valve cover, and workers with large steel wrenches unbolted the valve from the 12-inch pipe. I was surprised we were allowed to view the work at such a close distance. A tanker truck was brought in close, and a six-inch flexible hose was placed down in the soil pit. Gasoline immediately started roaring out, with the sandy soil being soaked to saturation. The tanker started sucking up the gas mixed with the sandy soil, and when the tanker was full, another tanker was brought in, but not before many gallons were lost to the earth. All of this was taking place only 50 feet away from a small creek that emptied into the O-At-Ka creek. Remember, this was 25 years before the creation of federal environmental controls.

We never thought the draining of the pipeline would take up to one hour, but the line was at a low point with it proceeding up a hill to the east and west. The 8000-gallon tankers were being brought in across our property from the south to the north and through four acres of newly planted Norway Spruce. The large trucks squashed the tiny spruce, so my Dad had a claim against the Atlantic Pipeline, which after much negotiation, they eventually paid.

Well, a new valve and seal were put in with a new valve cover, and to our surprise, the cover was secured with a large padlock. So, this was not only the end of our free Atlantic Hi-Arc gasoline but the end of my frequent inspection of the valve pit. We thought we might get an award for our discovery, but the pipeline company was not that appreciative. So be it for the Big Oil Companies!

Leaning Tower of Pisa

In 1950 my sister Eleanor and her husband Manny Costa started construction of their home at the corner of Route 19 and Cole Road next door to our farmhouse. The plan was to construct a spacious two-car garage that would have all the features of a home for five years or more until a regular home could be built just 50 feet away. This method was somewhat common after World War II for veterans returning home from the war and with insufficient cash to purchase a used home or construct a new one. During this period, there was also a shortage of materials due to the change from the war to peacetime. Bank loans also were tough to come by since veterans did not possess the cash for a mortgage down payment.

Manny and Eleanor bought a used home on Church Street in a section called Kansas and lived there for a few years until the garage/home was constructed on Warsaw Road. The foundation or footers were poured first with the help of my Dad, brother Al, and Manny. When it was time for construction of the walls and roof, all of the immediate relatives, including uncles, cousins, and in-laws, were called for a home raising day.

It was a beautiful Saturday morning in early June when about ten adult men arrived to start the build. The walls were to be constructed of cinder block, including a large cinder block chimney. Since this would eventually be converted into a garage, two large openings were left at the front of the building for garage doors. An electric powered cement mixer was started, and shovels of cement and sand were thrown into the mixer along with sufficient water to make cement, what we called "mud." Each worker knowing his skills took a position working in pairs, with one placing mortar on the block joints and the other placing the cinder block onto the mortar. The excess mortar would then be scraped away and wiped with a mason trowel.

Construction Begins

I had an essential job titled, "the water boy" and carried a bucket of cold water along with a metal dipper to each worker displaying beads of sweat from their brow in the hot sizzling sun. My Dad served as the "inspector" and commented to the dismay of his relative workers when mortar joints were crooked, too thin, or too thick. A plumb bob, a string with a weight attached, was used to align the walls and corners. In late afternoon, with much progress being made on the walls, two men started work on the cinder block chimney. I was running out of water and made another trip to the old farmhouse. On returning down the trodden path between our farmhouse and the new building, I happened to glance up and, to my utter surprise, witnessed a very slanted chimney. The two men on scaffolding were building a chimney at least 30 feet high that was listing at a dangerous angle. I immediately told my inspector Dad, who instructed the two anonymous met to come down from the scaffold and view this "leaning tower of Pisa." All of the men gathered to view this eyesore and, with a chorus of laughter, embarrassed the two relatives.

The Old Brown Table at dinner that evening echoed with laughter at this construction feat. By then, the two relatives had taken down the crooked chimney and were reconstructing it only this time with a good plum line. They had to wait for their dinner!

Fire in the Hole!

When growing up as a young teenager, I had a fascination with fireworks, and the Fourth of July was always an exciting time of the year. I was instructed by my Dad always to be careful with firecrackers. He told me stories at the Old Brown Table of growing up in Buffalo in the late 1890s and seeing kids blowing their fingers off with Cherry Bombs and Skyrockets. On Independence Day, you could hear ambulance sirens all day long from people being injured with these insane powerful unregulated fireworks. The story left quite an impression on me, so I always tried to be careful with the small firecracker by lighting the fuse and running for cover. However, what do you do when the firecracker is a dud and does not explode? How long do you wait before picking it up? You guessed right, not long for a young boy with no patience.

My introduction to the giant explosives did not occur until my brother-in-law, Manny Costa, was starting to build his house next door. The first job was to find water since there was no public water line two miles south of the village of Le Roy. My Uncle Bob Kelly said he could find water by using a divining rod made from a y-shaped cherry tree limb. The method is called dowsing, water divination, or water witching. He walked the field close to where the house would be built, holding the freshly cut tree limb with each hand grasping the two legs of the branch. As he walked, he suddenly exclaimed, "The y-branch is twisting in my hands, pointing downward." He then gave it to my brother Al who found the same forceful downward movement. I was astonished and related it to my Dad at the Old Brown Table that evening. But this was only the beginning of "fireworks" to find water.

Next, my Dad and Manny built a tripod out of three-inch diameter pipe, reaching about 15 feet high. Then they filled a ten-gallon can with molten lead, which was obtained from a relative that worked for the Buffalo Transit System. They would haul the heavy can to the top of the tripod with a rope and pulley system and let it fall freely to hammer a three-inch pipe with a pointed bullet nose into the ground. The bullet nose had several holes drilled into it so water could infiltrate the line. Then followed a cadence of up and down pounding of the pipe into the sandy-clay soil until reaching ten feet depth when water was poured into the pipe. A hand pump was attached, and they would pump to draw up water. Down another five feet, and they would try again, but all they got was a dry hole. Repeating the routine at 20 feet, 25 feet, 35 feet, but to their frustration, no water. Now there was a natural gas well just six hundred feet west of the attempted well that had been spewing some natural gas for several years. This area was known for natural gas deposits. But no natural gas was struck either!

Finally, since they had not struck water, they believed the holes at the bottom of the pipe could be plugged. That's when they went to Plan B; dynamite the hole. Manny's brother Christie worked at the local stone quarry and had access to dynamite. He was knowledgeable on the proper use of the dangerous substance, at least we all hoped he indeed had that knowledge. So, on a chilly October night in 1950, Christie arrived with sticks of dynamite, fuses, and igniter caps. I watched in excited wonder as he cut the dynamite into three-inch lengths, inserted a cap igniter with a 12-inch fuse, and covered it all with grease to protect it from the water. The explosive was dropped into the pipe, and as Christie yelled, "Fire in the Hole," we all ran toward the farmhouse. Boom went the charge, the ground shook, and a massive fountain of water sprang forth just like Old Faithful at Yellowstone. Now the hand pumping of the well was started again but no water. Christie increased the charge to four inches and repeated the process. Still no water. He raised the dynamite to six inches, and the explosion was so great that the old farmhouse next door trembled. No water! That is when the realization of a dry well set in and the remaining alternative was to contract with a water driller to obtain water. That did succeed, and they found water at around 65 feet, which turned out to be sulfur water, and Manny settled for what he could get.

All of this experience generated much conversation around the Old Brown Table, and Dad decided to have another well drilled for our farmhouse. The current well would go dry whenever there was a severe dry spell. So, a well driller was hired, and they sunk a six-inch pipe to a depth of 25 feet, providing an ample supply of water. However, it was sulfur water, which we were used to and did not give a second thought when satisfying your thirst. The Old Brown Table was also happy since we were not using dynamite to find water. The table had enough in being shaken to the core the previous month.

Model T Buzz

The Ford Model T was the first car that Dad purchased just before he married Mom in March 1916. For the first several years, he only used the Model T from late Spring until late Fall since the roads were not plowed, and the car was freezing to ride in with no heater. The horse and buggy or sleigh, if necessary, would be used to travel into Le Roy for work, church, or shopping. In 1936 Dad purchased his pride and joy 1936 Chevy four-door sedan and converted the Model T into a fun car without tires that could be run through the fields for a joy ride. The Buffalo gang, relatives from the great city of Buffalo, would come down in the summer and have a super time riding the Model T through the farm fields.

Buffalo Gang & Model T

The family in the Fall would prepare for the harsh winters with such activities as raking leaves, cleaning out the gardens, and putting up storm windows, just to name a few familiar duties. At our old farmhouse, there was an additional task in preparing wood for the kitchen stove. We had an unusual kitchen stove since it was a combination electric stovetop on the right side and a coal or wood burner on the left side. The Old Brown Table would feel its warmth on those cold wintry mornings when Mom would light a wood fire and then put in a shovel of pure black pea coal. The coal dust would spark and sizzle and burn off quickly. The tea kettle would go on the stove to heat water, which would be poured into a Drip-O-lator for a pot of Chase & Sanborn coffee. Then the skillet would go on the stove for eggs and bacon creating a substantial farm breakfast.

In the late 1930s, Dad stripped down the Model T, where only the engine, steering wheel, and chassis with four wheels remained. The engine drive shaft was connected to a 36-inch diameter circular saw, termed a buzz saw, which could cut thru tree trunks or limbs 12 inches in diameter. The improvised machine became a handy farm implement to saw tree trunks or waste lumber. Dad would never purchase any wood since plenty was available on our farm, but it had to be cut in the Fall and stacked in the basement of the farmhouse just below the kitchen.

Dad would hand crank the engine of the Model T with no muffler, and it would roar with such an outlandish deafening noise your ears would ring for an hour after the engine was shut down. I was terrified of this monster of a machine since I thought the buzz saw could fracture at any time and instantly kill the operator of the saw. The Old Brown Table heard me more than once express my fear of this machine. My Uncle Bob, who would always help Dad with the wood cutting, would tell the story around the Old Brown Table of how his brother was cut up the middle by a buzz saw fracturing in several pieces. So, I would stand back and fearfully watch my Dad stand directly in front of whirring saw and push the wood through like soft butter. Well, fortunately, we never had an accident, but we all did experience ringing ears until bedtime. That evening the Old Brown Table heard very loud conversation due to deaf buzz saw ears.

My Reckless Neighbors

Growing up in the country as a young boy had its advantages and drawbacks. One of the drawbacks was there were very few playmates close to my age. During the summer vacation months, one of my cousins would spend a week at my house, and sometimes I would do likewise at their home. When we did have neighbors with young boys, it was usually temporary since the family would be employed at the W. A. Johnson milk farm just a quarter mile down the road. On one occasion, when I was about thirteen years old, a family moved in with three boys named Sonny, Chuckie, and Donnie. Sonny was the most senior around the age of sixteen, while Chuckie and Donnie were a year or two under me.

Now to take you back to the 1940s and 50s, the current fad for young boys was cowboys demonstrated in hats, shirts, red neckerchief, pants, and of course, the six-gun and holster set. If you had a holster with two six guns, you stood out among the crowd. One summer day, when the above three neighbor boys visited me, they showed their pride and joy a toy six gun that was modified to fire 22 short bullets. Their Dad showed them how they could take the toy six-shooter revolving barrel, pour in molten lead, and drill out six holes to hold the 22-caliber short live cartridge. The firing pin was the toy gun hammer that would pull back from a finger on the trigger and strike forward to ignite the cap on the 22-caliber short. However, they told me that most of the time, it would not fire the cartridge.

I was astounded at this mod of a toy six-shooter, and at the same time, a fear startled me as to how such a toy gun could function safely as a standard gun. I did have enough sense to realize that the metal in a toy gun is quite fragile and could fragment on the explosive force of even a small 22 short. I suggested to them that this was probably not a safe gun, and they with pride agreed, and Sonny showed me where his gun had misfired by blowing the hammer back to where some of the pot metal had penetrated his right thumb. Then he proudly displayed a scar in his left shin where a 22-caliber bullet had entered last year from one of his brothers recklessly firing his toy gun.

As a result of this dangerous encounter, I tried to maintain my distance from my neighbor friends until one day, when I was riding my bike past their farmhouse, they called me back behind the farmhouse across the road from the Johnson milk farm. They were again playing with their guns while their Dad was milking the cows. I don't believe their Dad cared about gun safety but only encouraged the dangerous activity. They showed me with pride a new set of six-shooters, which they had recently modified from toy six guns that used to fire a roll of harmless caps. I intended to leave without insulting them when I turned around inside the barn and saw Chuckie striking something on a barn beam with a hammer. Being curious, I asked Chuckie if he was trying to bring down the barn. He laughed and showed me he was striking the cap of a 22-caliber live cartridge with the intent of firing it. I froze with fear and immediately uttered a goodbye while I jumped on my bike and rode home. I burst into the kitchen with the Old Brown Table and described what I had witnessed. From that time on, I was no longer allowed to have any contact with the reckless neighbors.

That said, I did ride to school with Donnie on the Le Roy Central school bus. One day I sat with him right behind the bus driver. He told me he wanted to show me something and drew out a real pistol from his lunch bucket. He was bringing it to school to show his classmates. Was it loaded, I wondered as he played with it showing off its attributes? When I arrived at school, I was terrified of the possibility of someone being shot. If I did not tell the Principle, Dr. Horr, I would be just as responsible for some student being injured or the unthinkable being murdered. But how can I report on a fellow student who was after all a neighborhood friend? After an agonizing hour, I told the teacher what I had witnessed, and she immediately sent me to the principle. I nervously informed Dr. Horr on what I had seen. He listened and very calmly told me to return to my class. Now I never heard what happened to Donnie with the real pistol, but I do know for sure that the Old Brown Table heard quite a tale upon returning home from school that afternoon.

Place of a Thousand Names

One of my favorite pastimes as a young lad was to hike on the W. A. Johnson farmland just to the west of our farm property across the B&O railroad tracks. You could start the hike at the junction of Cole Road and the B&O tracks and travel through the cow pasture, which held Johnson's milk cows and the terrorist bull. The property was protected by an electric fence to keep the cows inside, but it was also a challenge to us young boys to cross over the fence without being shocked. After making it over the fence without being shocked, we had to travel the length of the cow pasture, being always on the lookout for the bull and, at the same time, avoiding the cow flops of which there was always a considerable number. Upon reaching the far north side of the pasture, you had to cross a creek that flowed fast in the Spring and very slow in the Summer. There was a concrete railroad bridge crossing over the stream with the large number imprinted "1947", the date the bridge was constructed.

There was a large pond beside the pasture, which was a decent fishing spot for catching Bluegills. One day on the other side of the creek in bordering woods, I found a rusted-out lunch kit. Upon bringing it home to the farmhouse, my Mom thought it was from the 1930s when tramps would ride the rails during the Great Depression. She told me many a time the tramps would walk up the farm field to the farmhouse to ask for something to eat. Dad and Mom would always provide some food for these men who would travel the rails to find work. In my imagination, I could see those men in dirty torn clothing riding the rails, getting out of the boxcars by the pond, while the steam engine filled their tank with pond water. Then they would find a spot in the woods for a night's rest before the early morning train to catch an empty boxcar. The Old Brown Table heard many a tale about these men and the harsh life they were leading.

Author at Place of Thousand Names

Beyond the creek, there was a small hill you had to climb to reach another grove of trees. From here, there was a nice view of the creek and the pasture. Walking about twelve feet above the creek along a tree-lined ridge, you would come to a grove of Grey Birch trees where you could discover many names carefully carved into the grey bark. We always carried penknives and did our share of cutting into that tender grey bark. Of course, I could not resist and did the same with the initials "BB 51" for the year 1951. I found my Dad's initials, "JB 41," and others that I could not associate with anyone. We often wondered who the other carvers were and could only speculate by fitting a name to the grown fattened bark initials.

Well, I had to name this private place, so I came up with "The Place of a Thousand Names," although a thousand names were exaggerated since there were only ten or twenty. To a young boy, a thousand sounded a lot better. Beyond the Place of a Thousand Names, the path following the creek went downhill until you reached the O-At-Ka Creek, where the smell of algae, tadpoles, slate, and fresh running creek water entered a young boy's nostrils. Now that was living to be in a place that practically no one knew existed.

Several years later, in 1959, I met my future wife, Mary Ann, while in the Air Force at Wright Patterson Air Force Base in Dayton, OH. When we became serious in our relationship, I asked her to take a trip with me to Le Roy to meet my parents. In preparation, she got permission from her parents, and on Mother's Day weekend in 1959, we made the one-day trip to the homestead in Le Roy. While we were there, we took the short hike to my favorite spot, The Place of a Thousand Names, and there is where I proposed to Mary Ann. When we returned to the homestead and entered the kitchen, the Old Brown Table witnessed us informing my Dad and Mom that we were engaged. We were surprised that they were not surprised. They indeed saw the love we shared.

Whenever our family visited the homestead, Mary Ann and our four sons would hike back to that favorite place, and I would show them the names carved into the trees. Several years later, on June 29, 2007, Mary Ann and I, with our son Richard and his family, took that walk to The Place of a Thousand Names. We all carved our names into the trees and looked at my two carvings in 1958 and 1951. The 1951 carving was in a tree that was about ready to collapse into the creek due to 70 plus years. We were going to break it off and take it with us when I decided to allow it to return to dust, just like all of us will in due time.

I often wonder today if young boys still venture into those fields and woods and gleefully carve their names into those beautiful birch trees at the Place of a Thousand Names.

Salt Mine Oil

Would you believe that an abandoned salt mine could produce crude oil? Well, I can testify to the fact that it can. As a young lad, I would often ride my bike about a half-mile down Warsaw Road south of the old farmhouse to walk in the cow pasture where the Lehigh Salt Mine existed in the late 1800s. The salt mine was on the west side of Warsaw Road just beyond where the road crosses a small bridge and curves slightly to the south. My parents told me that a salt mine existed here sixty years ago and was abandoned when a low quality of salt was encountered during the first few years of operation. However, the fact of an inferior grade of salt was disputed. Many believed the mine was shut down because of the overproduction of salt in Genesee and Livingston counties.

On one of my visits to the salt mine site, I smelled a powerful pungent odor of oil as I approached the mine shaft. No buildings existed any more at the site since they were dismantled after the mine was shut down in 1893. The mine shaft was a large rectangular opening 13 by 24 feet with charred timbers caused by a fire some years past. The rectangular shaft opening was protected by a six-foot rusted chain link fence to prevent youngsters like me from plunging in and meeting my demise. In viewing the shaft opening about twelve feet down, you could see a brown liquid with stripes of yellow sulfur that gave forth a strong odor of crude oil. On viewing the oil, my mind started to wonder as to what use this stinking liquid could have for a young lad. Around that time, my cousin and I had constructed a shack about 500 feet west of the homestead red barn. We had moved a small cast iron stove from the barn to the hut to provide heat in the winter. That is when I had the brainstorm of getting some of this oil to heat the shack next winter.

But how do you extract oil from the mine shaft surrounded by a six-foot chain-link fence? Then it occurred to me to use a quart tomato juice can with a heavy string attached to the can. So back home I went, found a tomato juice can in the garbage, punched a hole near the top opening of the container and tied a long one quarter inch rope that I found in the red barn. Jumping on my bike with haste, I pedaled to the salt mine, crawled over with caution the barbed wire fence, and rushed to the shaft. Over the chain-link fence, I threw the tomato juice can with the rope attached. It sunk with a thud on the smelly oily surface and slowly filled up with crude oil. Then I hoisted the filled can to the top of the chain-link fence and slowly brought it over the top. I had found an empty five-gallon oil can in the barn, so I gradually filled the large can to about half full because the crude oil was very dense and heavy.

Well, that evening, the Old Brown Table heard of my day's adventure with my parents, brother, and sister listening with contained amusement. What was I going to do with this rancid oil I was asked? Well, heat my shack, of course when the weather turns cold in a few months. The few months flew by fast, and on a cold, snowy winter day, a boyhood friend and I made a trip to the shack carrying a newspaper, kindling wood from the woodshed, and the five-gallon can of crude oil. First, we placed the newspaper and kindling wood in the stove with an old pot on top of the wood and lit the fire that soon turned into a roaring blaze sending off an intriguing odor of burning wood. When the fire was well underway, we opened the top lid of the stove, and I poured in a sufficient quantity of crude oil, which ignited immediately pouring forth a black sooty smoke that we started to choke on. We opened the door, got a few gasps of breath, stood back, and admired the feat we had accomplished. No one in upstate western New York was heating with crude oil that day or likely never since. After a while, we became bored with our grand feat, and with the fire out, we closed the shack door and trudged through the beautiful white snow to the farmhouse carrying my precious five-gallon can of crude oil.

It was time for dinner at the Old Brown Table, and when we rushed into the kitchen and sat down, my Mom gave me the strangest look and asked where we got the black faces. What black faces did I wonder? Then Mom gave the ultimatum to wash up before we could touch our food. I rushed into the bathroom and saw with horror my blackened face caused, of course, by the burning crude oil. Then there was the terrible smell that our clothes put forth now requiring a complete change before we could eat a bite of that delightful homemade dinner. By the time we reached the Old Brown Table, everyone else was finished and happy we had not spoiled their dinner.

Next time we lit a fire in the shack cast iron stove, it was paper and wood only. But now what to do with the crude oil. That winter, my dad was going to plow the driveway with the doodlebug, and upon checking the engine oil found it needed about a quart. "Dad, I have oil taken from the salt mine," showing him the five-gallon can. Dad just laughed and told me he was not going to risk ruining his Ford Model A doodlebug with the unrefined oil. I did not know you had to refine oil and thought crude oil was just that, plainly CRUDE!

The Old Brown Table overheard another good laugh at the dinner table that evening. It was years later that I heard some teenage boys had lit the crude oil in the salt mine shaft, and it resulted in a significant oil fire that was difficult to put out. I have often wondered how much crude oil was in the mine shaft since it is 700 feet down. I don't believe we will ever know, not even the Old Brown Table.

Sky Snakes

On a warm June summer morning, I walked to the barn to take out my bicycle for a short ride down Cole road. It was a beautiful morning with a clear blue sky and a perfect day for a bike ride. The front of the barn had two garage doors, which were on overhead tracks that allowed the doors to be pulled open, permitting access and removal of vehicles as necessary.

I went to the door on the right and pulled the door on inside rollers completely open. From the corner of my eye, I saw something fall, and with quick instinct, I ducked to the left and was startled to see an 18-inch snake squirming on the barn floor. Immediately I thought, how could a snake crawl up to the top of the barn door and for what reason. As the snake coming to its senses escaped to a hole in the barn floor, I saw the possible route the snake took. There were some farm implements in the barn corner next to the garage door that would allow a snake to coil its way eight feet vertical to where it would reach the barn door tracks. The snake was apparently on the tracks when I opened the door causing the snake to lose its grip and come tumbling to the floor.

The remaining mystery was why would a snake take all of this effort to climb to the barn ceiling. Viewing the ceiling, consisting of wooden 2x8 rafters with crossbars to reinforce the rafters, I spotted a barn swallow bird nest with little chicks. Now the mystery was unveiled! The snake was heading to the nest to swallow up chicks for dinner. A lot of effort but the prize was worth it to a snake.

Well, for the duration of that summer and into the fall, every time I rolled back the barn doors to enter, I would move very slow looking for "Sky Snakes." I never did witness one again, but it sure made a good story at the Old Brown Table!

That Mysterious Silver Metal

When I was in my sophomore year at Le Roy High School, my primary interest was in math, physics, and chemistry. I was fortunate to have some excellent teachers that were not only good at teaching the subject but took a particular interest in their students. I grew up always curious about everything that came into my path from crayfish to rocks. One day I was looking at some unique arrowheads that my brother Frank had collected in the local area, and I believe some he found when he was stationed at Camp Gordon, GA, during World War II. In this small box of arrowheads were some mysterious pieces of silver metal that glistened in the sunlight. I started on a mission to find out the name of this metal ore and wondered if it was found locally,

Le Roy High School

although my dad did not believe so. Just think, maybe my brother discovered a valuable ore on our property or in the surrounding fields.

144

After school one day, I went to the Woodward Memorial Library next to the high school and found a few books on minerals. However, to my disappointment, none of the pictures matched what I had in my hand. Hence, the next day after school, I brought the shiny mineral to my biology teacher, Mr. Letko, along with a book that specified tests that could be run to identify minerals. I thought Mr. Letko would probably dismiss the action due to a lack of interest or time on his part in a young boy asking a lot of questions. But to my surprise, he took a genuine interest, and we started various tests using acids and various other chemicals that he had access to from the biology/chemistry storeroom. Well, after an hour of testing, we could not conclude as to what this mineral was or to its origin. I came home that afternoon, and at the Old Brown Table expressed my excitement on my experiments with Mr. Letko, which encouraged me to further my interest in the sciences.

Other teachers showed similar interests, such as my math teachers, Miss Fortmiller and Mr. James Perrone, and my chemistry teacher Mr. Sebastian Gangi. They always had time to answer questions and provide guidance on pursuing careers in the science field.

Later in life, I wondered why did Mr. Letko have such an interest in a curious young student, and now at the age of 84, I finally understand the reason. I learned you get a special feeling when you teach and mentor someone and share in their excitement of learning. You are participating in forming their future in reaching for the stars.

That Old Accordion Player

Over the years, the Old Brown Table heard joyous laughter, shouts of joy, and many times melodious sounds. In the mid-1940s, Billy was interested in learning to play the accordion, sometimes called the squeezebox. Billy had heard local musicians play the accordion since it was a choice instrument of Italian and Polish heritage. Dad visited Roxy's Music Store in Batavia, NY, and purchased a used 12-base accordion since the store manager suggested that a student should start with the basics before advancing to a larger instrument. Billy was a little disappointed since I wanted to go big time now.

Billy started taking accordion lessons from Tony Stella at his mother's home in Lime Rock just two miles east of Le Roy. The classes were one hour and started with learning notes, timing, and easy songs like Home Sweet Home. Billy was repeatedly told he must practice at least one hour per day so he would set up his music stand in the living room, take the accordion out of the small leather case and try his best to hit the right notes. The advancement was slow but steady to where he was ready for a 120-base accordion. The 120-base was the standard instrument used by entertainers in the industry.

Billy & 12 Base Accordion

Dad and Mom had faith in Billy continuing his music endeavor, so a purchase was made for an Italian 120-base accordion at the cost of $150 ($1700 in $2020). Since Billy was advancing, a new music teacher was sought. The new teacher was a blind man who lived in Batavia, NY, just ten miles to the west of Le Roy. Thus, I began five more years of lessons leading into playing those 1950 favorite songs of the day like Stardust; I'm Looking Over a Four-Leaf Clover, and the Beer Barrel Polka. The practice soon led to more complex renditions like the Parade of The Wooden Soldiers, Dizzy Fingers, and Lady of Spain.

In my high school senior year, the high school music and band teacher, Mr. William Lane, asked me to play in the concert high school band. I could not play in the marching band since it would be difficult to carry an accordion, pump the bellows, and march at the same time. I don't know for sure because I never tried that feat. One day Mr. Lane asked me to play a few of my more complex songs for him. I did not understand why until after I finished, he asked me to play a solo at the spring band concert in a few weeks. I was amazed, but I liked the idea. Halfway through the performance, I played my solo, Parade of the Wooden Soldiers at a breakneck pace with my fingers flying over the keys. When I finished, the audience came to their feet and continued to clap, wanting an encore. But I was not prepared for an encore, so I rapidly took my seat, and the band finished the concert.

Soon my Dad received a request for me to play at a church in Le Roy and without informing me committed me to the date. On a warm Wednesday summer night, he took me to the Second Baptist Church at 73 Myrtle Street. When I walked in, I was shocked to see all black people and did not realize that the Second Baptist was organized for the black community. I had memorized a few songs at this time and was going to play the song Down Yonder, which I by some imagination thought would be appropriate. The sight of the all-black congregation rattled me, and when I was ready to play, I froze and could not remember a single note. In desperation, I pulled the second song from memory, the Beer Barrel Polka. Now you can believe for a Wednesday night church service that was a first. I must have been the comment of that congregation for weeks to come, and indeed I was never asked to perform there again. Well, the Old Brown Table never heard a word from my Dad that evening, so I just assumed that all went well. Ignorance is bliss!

The Woodward Legacy

The Old Brown Table witnessed many discussions after Edith Hartwell Woodward's death on October 8, 1955, about the Ernest and Edith Woodward legacy. Since many years and a few generations have now passed, the current Le Roy residents probably don't know about the generosity of the Woodward's and the positive effect on this small town in upper New York State.

The legacy started in the early 1900s with the meager beginning of Jell-O production from the Genesee Pure Food Company, which later merged with the Postum Cereal Company to form the Jell-O Company. This company was a steady employer for Le Roy for sixty plus years, reaching 600 employees at its peak until eventually the plant was closed in 1964 and operations moved to Dover, DE. The founder, Orator F. Woodward, ran the company only a few short years until his health failed in 1905, and his oldest son, Ernest, with his mother Cora, took over operations.

At the close of the 1920s, Ernest retired from active business operations when General Foods took on the management. At the young age of 28, he began a period of philanthropy with his wife Edith that would continue for the rest of his life. It included gifts to individuals, businesses, hospitals, schools, and municipalities. Upon the death of Ernest in April 1948 and Edith in October 1955, the last will and newspaper reports described the most memorable gifts. The list below is an attempt to capture the main portion of the Woodward's philanthropy.

Edith & Ernest Woodward

- Early in the 20th century, Ernest Woodward purchased Ingram College and gave the site to the community for the use of the Union Free School. In 1906 four pieces of residential property on Wolcott Street were donated as a site for the Wolcott Street Grammar School, a value of $31,500.
- Ernest Woodward purchased several hundred acres in the North Woods northeast of Le Roy along the O-At-Ka Creek. He established a game preserve, which later was given recognition by the State Conservation Commission.
- Ernest Woodward was a member of the Letchworth Park Commission for several years and had an active part in the expansion and improvement of the park.
- The Grandstand at the high school athletic field was donated in 1929 to provide a fitting background for the future library.

- The Orator Woodward family donated the Woodward Memorial Library in 1930 with a substantial endowment of more than $250000. Later in 1948, $300000, and in 1955 an additional $30000 trust fund was established wherein the income was to be used for operation and maintenance of the library.
- A $45000 gift was made to the University of Rochester in 1939, providing research in epilepsy.
- A large financial investment in the Le Roy Post Office building, starting with the donation of the site, followed with a modification of the rooflines and the addition of a clock tower. This donation was an addition to federal funding since Ernest Woodward wanted the building to be a credit to the village at its completion in 1938.
- Remodeling of the interior of St. Mark's Church in 1946, of which Ernest was a communicant and former vestryman.
- The Donald Woodward estate was donated to the University of Rochester in 1946. The estate was designated as the Edith Hartwell Clinic for the rehabilitation of spastic children. The gift was accompanied by a substantial sum for furnishing and equipping the center.
- The original home of Ernest and Edith Woodward, the J. G. Gilfillan residence, was donated to the American Legion in 1945.
- Donations to Genesee Memorial and St. Jerome Hospital each receiving $50000 for their building funds and later an additional $250000 gift to Genesee Memorial. Edith Woodward also gave a special gift of $50000 to Genesee Memorial on March 9, 1950, to start a $300,000 fund drive.
- The University of Rochester was granted a gift of $1,500,000 for research in the medical sciences.
- The donation of the former A. W. Lawrence residence and farm of 47 acres on South Street road to the Le Roy Central School District. The gift was for a future athletic field and park, subsequently named Hartwood Park. The

gift included a substantial sum for fitting and lighting the field and the construction of a field house. A trust fund of $75000 was established for the maintenance of the athletic field. Later this would become the site for the new High School.
- Endowment fund for the University of Rochester $5,600,000, Rochester Institute of Technology $1,200,000, Salvation Army $400,000, Rochester Humane Society $400,000, Seeing Eye Inc. $400,000 and $50,000 for the Children's Home in Batavia.
- The Woodward residence on East Main Street was donated to the University of Rochester. Later the university decided not to use the mansion or land, and according to the will, it was required to tear down the estate and sell the land for construction of private residences.

When the author graduated from Le Roy Central School in 1953, the Hartwood Park bequest was made known to the community. Our senior class of 1953 decided the O-At-Kan yearbook be dedicated to Edith Woodward because of her generous gift to the school district, and we wanted to place a picture of her in the yearbook. When serving as the photographer for the yearbook, I was informed about taking her portrait. I was thrilled about that possibility since I had met her several times through my Dad's employment at her residence. When I came home from school and had my milk and cookie at the Old Brown Table, I excitedly told Mom I was going to photograph Edith in a few days for the yearbook. However, Edith informed the school that she was very appreciative of the dedication but refused to have her picture shown. Instead, I took a picture of the empty field where Hartwood Park would eventually be located. The Hartwood athletic field was opened in the fall of 1955 with night lighting and high school football. The football team sent a message to Edith in the hospital, conveying their appreciation for the gift of the field, and they would pray for her speedy recovery. She died within a few days of that thank you note.

LRGN: 6-20-1917; 4-22-1948; 10-8-1955; 8-19-2018.

Unusual Table Foods

Over 90 years, the Old Brown Table witnessed the presentation of various delectable delights, although some could be placed in the mysterious category. One day a large box of fruit arrived from Los Angeles, CA, shipped from my Uncle Bill and Aunt Francis Ireland. As the box was opened, we discovered a sheet of instructions identifying the fruit and how to prepare for consumption. Now there was the familiar orange and grapefruit that Dad and Mom could buy locally, but we then discovered some strange looking fruits that we did not recognize.

First, there was the avocado a strange-looking greenish-black fruit that we thought at first was spoiled until the thick skin was peeled as per instruction, and the smooth yellow inside was exposed. The family gathered around the Old Brown Table was anxiously waiting for a sample and, when tasted, got mixed reviews. Next came the artichoke displaying the many thick pale green leaves. The instructions said to pull each leaf off the choke and hold the pointed end between your fingers. Then drag the sprig between your teeth and if you desire to dip the leaf in olive oil to enhance the taste. The procedure seemed like a lot of work to just get a small taste of fruit, so the reviews were not so good. The mangos were tried next, and there was some difficulty in taking the fruit away from the strange flat pit. The orange color and the sweet taste provided a decent review but was judged not as good as a natural fresh apple. The family at the Old Brown Table, although excited about their new knowledge of California fruits, was ready to return to the familiar New York State apples, cherries, and pears.

In late October 1951, preparations were in high gear for the marriage of my sister Mary to Francis Morgan. The date was set for Saturday, November 3, and the family was very busy with all of the last-minute details. The reception was to be held at the Broadway Hall in Lime Rock with plans for a band and various snack foods. Mary saw a recipe for a delicious finger food that was quite simple to prepare. So, on Friday night before the wedding, we all gathered around the Old Brown table to prepare this snack. Several boxes of saltines and deviled ham were purchased along with mayo and a few spices. After mixing the deviled ham with the mayo and spices, the mixture was spread on the saltines and carefully placed in a container separated by wax paper. Of course, we sampled a few, and we thought these would indeed be a hit at the reception.

The next morning the containers were taken from the back kitchen where it was cold enough to prevent spoilage. Someone thought they would sample one before taking the snacks to the reception hall. To our surprise, the saltines were very soggy, destroying not only the appearance but the taste as well. The main wedding snack was a complete failure, and all had to be discarded. However, all was not lost when plan B went into effect with a quick trip to the grocery to purchase potato chips and pretzels and a good story to tell at the reception.

What is That Horrible Noise? The Doodlebug

In the 1940s and 50's it was a common practice to build your own farm tractor that would meet the summer need for preparing medium-size gardens and in the winter plowing snow from the driveway. They would take an old car, such as a Model A Ford or a Chevy, and strip it down with modifications to make a Doodlebug. My dad's Doodlebug was made from a 1929 Model A Ford coupe called a "Roadster." The body metal, including the fenders, running boards, doors, and the remainder of the body, would be removed, exposing the naked frame. One foot was then cut off from the rear of the frame to shorten the vehicle. Then the transmission, torque tube, and the

Al Plowing with Doodlebug

universal rear end were removed and replaced with a Model A truck transmission and a truck rear end. This modification provided a lower gear ratio for a slower speed and more traction for pulling a plow or plowing snow. The only thing left on the frame was the engine, radiator, front headlights, lever brakes, cowl with firewall and gas tank, steering wheel, instrument panel, brake & clutch pedal, and of course, a seat for the driver. What was left was an actual vehicle that made a loud noise since, for some reason, the muffler was left off.

Every time the Doodlebug was started up, The Old Brown Table could hear the bang-bang of its four cylinders firing off, and if you drove it or stood close, the sound was deafening. My dad would allow me to ride with no seat, just squatting down by the dashboard and let the exhaust, smoke, dust, and that unbelievable sound penetrate my body. That was living for a young country boy!

Who Can Forget the Laughter?

Over many years the Old Brown Table witnessed many occasions of family and friend's laughter. When friends or relatives would visit, they often would smoke pipes or cigarettes since smoking tobacco was prevalent in the 1940s and 1950s. The health risks were not completely known at that time until research showed the risk to the human body caused by the ingredients from tobacco smoke. I would love playing a trick on a relative by taking one of my brother's cigarettes and placing a small sliver of wood dipped in gunpowder into the end of the cigarette. My brother would hand the cigarette to my relative, and when they would light up the end of the cigarette, it would explode with a loud bang, causing no injury, of course.

We also would have fun with table tricks such and balancing a fork and spoon on the edge of a glass of water, a gravity-defying stunt. Then there were the eyeglasses with a large rubber nose attached that would, without hesitation, generate laughter to the audience around the Old Brown Table. Then who could forget the dancing teeth that you could wind up and they would chop, chop away?

Of course, the adults would play cards, an ordinary game of Pedro, or the more complex Canasta. The card games would always be accompanied by laughter and yelling when someone had a decent hand or a bad one.

In the 1950s, Weegie (Ouija) boards were popular. The family would gather around the Old Brown Table, and one would place their hand on the plastic or wood pointer. While everyone was quiet, they would ask the Weegie board a question, and the person's hand on the pointer would start moving toward the alphabet or numbers to deliver a message. As a child, I was intrigued by the mystery of the pointer as it would move and spell out a message. What mysterious force was present that could answer questions? Well, in time, I suspected my older sister or brother was providing the answers by moving the pointer to correct letters. Indeed, a silly game, but fun nonetheless.

A late-night lunch usually followed good times at the table that my Mom would provide. Cheese and crackers, liver sausage, cold cuts, pigs' feet, nuts, and desserts. Adults would have their beer or wine and the children their soda pop. All would eat to their heart's content, and I never saw anyone ask for a Tum.

How could you not remember the Old Brown Table clown? Uncle Bill Ireland fit the role completely. All you had to do was look at him, and he would make a remark with that silly grin on his face, and all would break out laughing. There was a style about him that was astonishing to see. When we had corn on the cob, he would cut the corn off because he had dentures and could not bite down on the kernels. Of course, he would remind everyone by partially removing his dentures. If we became silent at the table, he would start kidding someone about a recent event, and everyone would burst out laughing.

One must not forget my Uncle Bob and Aunt Katie Kelly. The Kelly's never had any children, so she was always very kind to her nieces and nephews handing out candy, small toys, and sometimes old coins she had collected. She always carried a black leather handbag with her wherever she went. One day she pulled out a glass container that was full of money. I found out later that this was their life savings. She would not trust her money in the bank because they lost their entire savings in the 1929 Market Crash when thousands of banks failed. No Federal Deposit Insurance Corporation had been established yet.

There is another part of the story that the Old Brown Table witnessed with the Kellys. If Uncle Bob had too much of my father's wine, Katie would remind him in front of all that he had enough.

Uncle Bob always sat at the table stone-faced without a single reply and would accept another glass of wine. Katie would follow with a sharp remark like, "You Old Boozer." The rude comment would create a silence but shortly followed with laughter by someone saving the moment. Oh, how the Old Brown Table remembers!

You Sliced Off the Fenders?

My sister Mary graduated from the Rochester Institute of Technology with a degree in Arts & Sciences. For a few years, she worked in Rochester at Eastman Kodak, supporting the World War Two effort. It was challenging to obtain a job after the war working as an artist until she finally found a job at the Mason Seal company in Batavia, NY. She was able to put her art skills to work, creating seals that would identify a product or the company.

Dad let her use his prize 1936 Chevy Sedan to travel back and forth to Batavia, which is ten miles west of Le Roy. Monday through Friday, Mary would take Cole Road through Jug City to Bater Road and then Route 5 west to Batavia. After passing Prole Road, the four-lane state highway would rise over a moderate hill and crest at Devil's Rock. The Devil's Rock was a unique limestone rock formation that looked like a giant toadstool, which was carved out by the glaciers during the Ice Age. The local folklore was the Devil chased the Indian around the rock, trying to unsuccessfully catch him, resulting in wearing down the middle of the stone.

One winter morning on Mary's trip to work driving the 36 Chevy, it was snowing very hard, and the windshield was clogging up with snow and ice to where she could hardly see anything. There were very few cars on the road and she was determined to reach the Mason Seal office for her workday. After passing Prole Road, she started up the grade of the hill trying to keep the car in the right lane, although she was not sure where she was with visibility nearly zero. Suddenly she saw a large truck directly in front of her so she instinctively pulled the car to the left. The 36 Chevy responded but not fast enough, and she struck the truck's driver's side with a loud crash, shaking the Chevy to the core. She swung past the vehicle and, with horror, realized she had hit the left side of a New York State snowplow, hitting the plow blade on the left side. Fearfully not wanting to stop, she continued until she was able to pull into a gas station. Upon exiting the car and viewing the right side, she discovered two fenders cleanly sliced by the outer edge of the snowplow blade. The fenders were hanging on just enough to make it to and from work that snowy day.

When Dad returned from work that late afternoon, he saw the right front and rear fenders barely hanging to the body of the car. He came in the kitchen and at the Old Brown Table heard Mary relate the details of her morning accident. Dad did not get angry but expressed gratitude that she had fortunately escaped injury. He did caution her, however, not to travel in such dangerous conditions since there had been several accidents that morning. Dad took the 36 Chevy to a welder in Le Roy, where the fenders were once again attached to the body. Mary had her first lesson in driving in the harsh upper New York state winters, as witnessed by many a tale at the Old Brown Table.

"Make a joyful noise to the Lord, all the earth;
Break forth into joyous song and sing praises!"
Psalm 98:4

Chapter Six

1960 To 1970 Old Brown Table Tales

A Day of Adventure at Grandma's House

There were such a variety of things to do at Grandma Browns. Since boys like to climb trees, there were some old apple and pear trees loaded with branches that the grandchildren wanted to climb. Now, Uncle Al had planted some smaller dwarf apple and pear trees, and the boys were warned not to climb these trees since they were more fragile. Now how do you make a boy listen to not climb a tree? Richard could not resist climbing regardless of his brother's warnings. When he reached the upper limbs, they heard a loud crack and down came the branch, Richard and all. At that moment, Richard made a pact with his brothers not to tell anyone. A slightly different approach than George Washington!

Sometimes the four brothers just enjoyed playing the old favorite kick the can since there were many places to hide around the farmhouse, red barn, and chicken coup. During one game Frank found a secluded spot by the chicken coup where no one could see him. But to his surprise, one of the brothers spotted him, and Frank made a fast sprint toward the can in the driveway. However, as soon as he jumped out of his hiding spot, he lost his footing and collided with an iron one-inch post that had sharp tangs on the top caused by driving it hard into the ground. His hand hit the top of the bar, and the short tangs dug into his hand with an immediate gush of blood. In his horror, he ran to the farmhouse yelling in pain that he was hurt and needed speedy aid. Well, Dad and Mom had been used to accidents such as these raising four boys and knew how to administer the first aide to stop the bleeding, apply antiseptic and a tight bandage. But upon examining the culprit pipe, it appeared a dark rusty brown, which would likely cause a severe infection. Without further discussion, Dad and Mom put Frank in the car, and a quick trip was engaged to St. Jerome's Hospital. After a short wait, Frank was examined, given a Tetanus injection much to his objection, insurance papers filled out, and within two hours returned to Grandma's. The Old Brown Table heard the full story of the accident with Grandma informing Uncle Al to remove the rusty iron post immediately.

One day Robert spotted a small iron horse standing on the top of the clothesline T-bar support. He wanted that cast iron horse but could not reach it, so he asked his brother Rich if he could get the horse for him. Now the only way Rich could grasp the horse was on Robert's back. So, Robert, although two years younger than Rich, supported Rich on his back and, sure enough, was able to take down the iron horse. Immediately Rich ran into the house, and by the Old Brown Table announced he had found a cast iron horse out by the clothesline. Little Robert just silently watched to see his horse galloping away.

Uncle Al loved to eat shelled peanuts at the Old Brown Table, cracking the shell with fragments spreading on the table and onto the floor. At Easter, he would overdose on hard-boiled eggs after peeling the eggshell and covering the egg with salt. His favorite time at the table was smoking his pipe or hand-rolled cigarettes.   On one occasion, he was given homegrown tobacco from a friend. Rather unusual since tobacco does not naturally grow in upper New York State. He decided to chew the tobacco, but apparently, the juice got to his sensitive stomach. The boys witnessed their uncle turning a light green at the Old Brown Table leading to a rush to the kitchen sink to release all in a violent moment. The unpleasant incident was followed by a comment from Grandma saying, "I told you so, but you wouldn't listen!"

Now Grandma always used a large teakettle she kept on the stove to heat water for making tea and for general cooking. Now the teakettle was very old and had scratches and dents on the sides. If one were to remove the lid and view inside, you would see a thick layer of orange material. Now the water from the outside well was considered hard water and had a pungent smell of sulfur. When boiled, the minerals in the water would be deposited into teakettle. One day at the Old Brown Table, Grandma told the boys that the old teakettle had sprung a leak. The boys thought they would get a trip to town to buy Grandma a new teakettle but were surprised to hear Grandma exclaim, "I can fix it!" She told the boys that the kettle needed a little maintenance, so she took a screwdriver and started chipping the orange lime from the bottom of the kettle. After removing the chunks of orange lime, she filled the teakettle with hard tap water and placed it back on the stove burner. "Grandma, the kettle will leak" the boys exclaimed. Grandma replied, "Just a little. When the water boils, the kettle will seal itself again." The boys did wonder what the hard sulfur water did to their insides, but they knew their Dad had lived there for many years and not yet turned orange.

One day there was a water leak from one of the pipes in the bathroom. At the Old Brown Table, Grandma told the boys she could fix that. They followed her into the bathroom, and she asked Richard for his bubble gum. Richard, with a puzzled face, gave the gum to her. Grandma placed the gum on the small leak on the pipe and confidently told them the leak was fixed. Yes, indeed, it was! Now there was some magic in that gum.

After a hot sticky autumn day of running circles around the barn, fruit trees, and fields of weeds, we would settle into the sunset. The evening breeze would carry the sound of crickets and the hollow hum of passing cars through the front door screen as we gathered in front of the TV. Grandma and Mom could be heard washing dishes while Uncle Alfred dried and put away. Before we were allowed to relax before the console TV, Mom would march us into the big claw iron tub to scrub away layers of stone dust, weedy burrs, and salty summer sweat. Clean, refreshed, and in our PJ's, we would scatter across the family room floor and laugh ourselves silly to the cornball country humor of Hee Haw, Petticoat Junction, or Green Acres. After the kitchen cleanup, Grandma, Alfred, Mom, and Dad would join us for the Lawrence Welk Show. As Bobby and Cissy danced and sang before us, Grandma would rock calmly in her chair and drift off. Her nap was her well-earned repose following a busy afternoon in a still, hot, country kitchen. It was there Grandma would cook up what was always a simple but delicious dinner of baked beans, drop biscuits with warm butter, and ham with homemade chili sauce on the side. Her canned pears in sweet syrup, dotted with maraschino cherries, usually found its place on the table as well. Strawberry shortbread with fresh whip cream would follow, or a scoop of Neapolitan ice cream with drizzles from a just-opened can of Hershey syrup.

When the evening entertainment ended, we would settle into dusty deep grooves of bedding, forged by generations before us, in the dark corners of tiny connected upstairs rooms. There, we would first giggle and joke, then simmer into our slumber, listening to the song of the gentle conversation below us. The ebb and flow of small talk would rise through the center floor vent, casting its checkered shadow on the ceiling above. Uncle Alfred and Grandma would bring Dad up to speed with the local news, dropping names of who had married, loved, lived, and died in Le Roy during his absence. As the final cast of the sunset surrendered to soft blue stars, we would drift off, reliving the day's adventures, secure in the love surrounding that Old Brown Table.

Ref: Robert Baroncinni (Brown), Frank Brown (Grandchildren).

Christmas at Grandma Browns

Christmas time at Grandma's was always something special for our family to look forward to each year! I remember well the smell of the fresh-cut Christmas tree in the living room, which filled the house with the aroma of fresh pine. Uncle Al was in charge of finding the tree in the woods behind the house and chopping it down. No tree farms or artificial trees when you can take one for free, with a bonus bird nest. The tree was always decorated with the old school ceramic string lights of many colors, lots and lots of tinsel and precious hand-made ornaments from family and friends. And there was extended family and friends ever stopping by and wishing a season's greetings, bringing cheer and making memories. One-time, Ronnie Hawkins and Richard Costa walked in the house in full USAF uniform and sat at the Old Brown Table. Wow, were they sharp!

As a young boy, a favorite time of mine included the many Christmas sweets and treats that filled the Old Brown Table. As the adults sat in the living room enjoying each other's company with casual conversation, the younger cousins would circle the kitchen table, enjoying all-night grazing of the assorted holiday delicacies. The treats included iced cookies, chocolate fudge, snickerdoodles, Santa snacks, peanut brittle, boxed candies, shelled nuts, and the necessary nutcracker. And how could I forget the bourbon balls that cleared my sinus perfectly every time and of course I only took one.

Brown Boys & David

A white Christmas, a common occurrence for upstate New York, was always a little extra special. Snow forts and snowball fights were always a great time with cousin David, who always found himself alone in his fortress, outnumbered and waging war against cousins Frank, Rich, Bob, and Chris. Yet it always seemed that David would win the day. We would stay outside so long in the cold that it seemed our face and hands would never thaw out. After many pleas from our parents to come inside where it was warm, we would fill the back room with our snowy boots, gloves, coats and scarves. After entering the warm kitchen, we would sit around the kitchen table where we would be greeted by Grandma's hot cocoa, which was always the best cup of hot chocolate in the world. The perfect ending to Christmas at Grandmas was the year when the news reported that large snowfalls had closed the toll road back to Ohio, met by cheers and dancing by my brothers and me! An extra day (or maybe two!) at Grandmas! It seemed that we never wanted it to end.

Now in the summer, there were apple fights since there were two large apple trees that produced a waste fruit since the trees were not maintained. The small green apples, usually containing wormholes, were the ideal weapons that could be hurled at top speed to your opponent. Of course, they would hurt on impact, but this was not a deterrent to a good fight. Unfortunately, the four Brown boys would gang up on David and give him quite a struggle. David always held his own and with good cheer.

My brothers and I are so blessed by these delightful memories around the Old Brown Table.

Ref.: Richard W. Brown (Grandchild).

Cookies and Milk

As a child, I always looked forward to visiting my Grandma, Grandpa, and Uncle Al, who lived with them in their home in Le Roy, NY. The drive from Buffalo seemed long to me back then, and I always looked forward to giving them hugs and running to the old flowered cookie jar in the kitchen near the Old Brown Table. Grandma Brown usually had it filled with homemade cookies, and molasses was my favorite. The cookies, of course, we're always accompanied by a glass of cold milk, but in the winter, Grandma would make us a cup of hot chocolate with a giant marshmallow on it. My Mom and dad would sit at the Old Brown Table and talk to Grandma while my sisters and I would run and play with our cousins. Sometimes we would go upstairs in the red barn, where there was an old wicker wheelchair and we would take turns pushing each other in it.

Other times we would go back to the creek before the evergreen trees got too big, and prevented us from finding our way back to it. When inside the house, we would go upstairs and play hide and seek and peer downstairs through a heat register in the floor that was above the kitchen and the Old Brown Table. These were open heat vents, and you could see downstairs. It was right near the table so we could listen to our parent's conversation. Grandma was always laughing. The best of times for my sisters and me.

Ref: Janice Morgan-Youngman (Grandchild).

Ghostly Children at Play

The homestead on Warsaw Road just outside of Le Roy had its share of history. Built by Great Grandpa Charles Baroncini, this house was born from not one, but two company tenant homes. The small tenant homes were purchased from the Lehigh Salt Mine in 1903. Charles had them horse-drawn a quarter-mile north to the Warsaw Road plot, joining them at a 90-degree angle to make a single-family home. One can only wonder how many previous immigrant families filled these homes with playful children and their exhausted, hard-working parents.

The Baroncini home was small, but warm and inviting as farmhouses should be. The Old Brown Table occupied nearly half of the kitchen. The close kitchen spacing was never a detriment, but instead a conduit of warm conversation between any who sat at the table. Generations shared a familial closeness that can be lost in the modern kitchens of today.

All bedrooms but one filled the upper level of the home. The "Master Suite," a small room behind the kitchen stove wall, was the bedroom for Charles and Mary Baroncini and later Jack and Nellie Brown. At the farthest end of the home from the kitchen, beyond the family room, rose a narrow flight of stairs. Set against the back wall, they beckoned a climb to anyone who started upon their worn flights. With no room to spare for such luxuries as hallways and bathrooms, the "upstairs" consisted of four simple bedrooms, daisy-chained so that one could not enter the farthest room without first passing through the previous three. In the 1960s and '70s, Alfred was the sole remaining child of Nellie and Jack to occupy a bedroom

Brown Homestead

there. His was the first entered, adjacent to the stairway, with no wall of privacy between his bed and the ascending stairs.

No upper room was spared from oddly angled ceilings. The bedrooms pushed their tops to their limits, pressing against the inner plaster ceiling of the roof above. Doorways between rooms followed the contoured peak of the roof, the only space elevated enough to allow an adult to pass through erect. Most bedframes were whitewashed tubular iron, hospital-style, with no embellishment. Wide plank battleship grey floorboards suspended these rooms above the kitchen and family room below, with glossy waxed linoleum covering the path of traffic between each room. The walls and slants were adorned with brittle green paper, fighting gravity and time with irregular cracks fingering paths through faded creamy white floral patterns.

The third room in the chain was one of the brightest. The corner afforded this room with windows overlooking the back garden, barn, and driveway. In this bedroom, during the wash-water grey transition when dusk still fought with the dawn, before the first chirp of birds and Grandma's muted kitchen clatter below, her grandson Bobby would awaken to visitors in his room. Two school-age children would appear from the shadows in cinematic fashion. They would quietly chase one another around the foot of the bed, softly giggle, and occasionally settle at the bed's edge beyond Bobby's feet. There he would curiously watch them as they watched him. The two children would face each other, shoulders perpendicular to the iron bed frame, and whisper in their playmate's ears. Their heads would turn, fingers pointing in recognition of Bobby's presence, before conversing again with cupped hands to the other's ears, muting their secret tales. They were silhouettes, formed of the same transitional grey mix between the black of night and the welcome of day. As mysterious and ghostly as they appeared, Bobby never reacted with fright, but rather with simple observation. They were enjoyable to watch, posed no threat, and would fade as the light of morning and aromas of bacon and eggs from the kitchen below would overtake them. It never occurred to Bobby to share the presence of his early morning visitors with his family. They were just a part of Grandma's home to him, sharing space with dusty corners, faded wallpaper, and the distant snores of Uncle Alfred two bedrooms away.

Now his brother Chris in his own words had a very similar version of the two ghostly children as follows. I'd find myself awake in the middle of the night for no reason. The room would be pitch black and silent. The house faced a busy road, and the passing trucks would light up the dark room and break the dreary silence. If I listened, I could hear my Dad and Uncle Al snoring in unison; if one was off sync the other would catch up, like crickets in the summer time. That sound was the only comfort I had, other than being able to see my parents in that adjacent small bedroom. And, somewhere between the snoring and the flashing truck lights, on the first night and always on the first night, I'd look towards the end of the bed to see the outlines of two small boys, colorless like a coloring book. Standing. Staring. One would lean over to whisper to the other; sometimes pointing at me. A low, and delicate and inaudible whisper. I had no idea what they were saying or why they were pointing, but I can remember this as young as 5 or 6. I only had enough sense to cover my head up, not think about it and fall back to sleep. It never came up and I think my child senses knew to forget about it pretty quickly. I was not scared about going to bed or worried about the "ghosts" with each subsequent visit to Grandma's. It would just happen visit after visit. I would forget until the next time, same two boys, same whispers and pointing.

Decades later, as an adult, Bobby (now Bob) sat around the kitchen table in Chandler, Arizona, on Halloween night with his wife Sylvia, brother Chris and his fiancé Beth. The timely conversation turned to ghost stories. Chris randomly shared a long-ago memory of two pre-dawn visitors to the bedroom above Grandma's kitchen. He described their playful scampering around the bed, the whispering of long-forgotten words, and the pointing and giggling directed at him as the morning light entered the room from those same corner windows. As with Bob, Chris had never felt compelled to share this experience before that Halloween night. His story turned the room silent, with prickled skin and hairs raised in alarm as Bob mirrored Chris's account of the same shadowy visitors. The unexpected convergence of these memories left them bewildered at best. The experience was no coincidence and had no explanation for the never before shared similarities. Now the Old Brown Table must have certainly witnessed the existence of these two mysterious figures. If it could only talk!

Ref: Robert Baroncinni, Christopher Baroncini (Grandchildren).

Grandma Brown's Hot Chocolate

A treat that was shared many times at the Old Brown Table was Grandma Brown's hot chocolate. Nobody knows how she made that hot chocolate, except it was always in a pan on the electric stove with exceptional cocoa and whole milk (maybe she slipped in a little cream). The electric stove was a hybrid of electric burners on one side and a two-burner wood or coal stove on the other side. When Grandpa Brown purchased the stove, he was told the company had stopped making them in 1950. It worked well for the Browns since it was convenient to heat the kitchen in the early morning for those cold winters in upper New York State. Grandma would start a fire early on those cold winter mornings with kindling wood laid on a newspaper from a bucket behind the stove. She would then control the stove damper to obtain maximum air for the fire. After the wood fire was well underway, she would add black pea coal using a small hand shovel with a responding crackle and sparks flowing up the chimney. The stove fire started warming the old farmhouse kitchen and was ready for any food preparation for the entire day.

All of Grandma Brown's grandchildren remember her hot chocolate, usually accompanied by crackers and sharp yellow cheese. When our family would arrive from Ohio on Friday night, they were always greeted with hot chocolate. When the Brown, Morgan, and Costa grandchildren played outside in the snow to where their bodies were practically frozen and wet, they would remove their wet clothes in the back kitchen and warmly greeted by Grandma's hot chocolate. The hot chocolate was sometimes accompanied by a homemade cookie from the flowered cookie jar that never seemed to go empty. Peanut, chocolate, sugar, and M&M cookies were the usual fare. But the highlight was the Hot Chocolate at the Old Brown Table!

Ref: Christopher W. Baroncini (Brown) (Grandchild).

Grandma Brown's Magic Kingdom

There are many times I'm filled with nostalgia when I think of Grandma Brown and her homestead on Warsaw Road. Today I think of it as Grandma Brown's Magic Kingdom, where there exist countless happy memories to be cherished for a lifetime. I remember walking up to Grandmas through the path between our houses, sometimes finding wild strawberries along the way in the weeds. In the spring there would be daffodils to pick for her and in August pears from the pear tree at the end of the path. I can picture Grandma with her apron on, quart jars lined up on the Old Brown Table and her hands tirelessly peeling and canning pears. Every pear was perfectly placed inside each jar with a fork so they looked pretty when finished with a maraschino cherry. I don't know how she did all of her cooking with so little, or I should say no counter space. That is where the Old Brown Table provided sufficient space for a task like canning.

If I were bored at home, I'd walk up to Grandmas, and we would sit at the table with a cup of tea and cookies and chat. Alfred would usually come out from his nap, sit down, bring his pipe in the ashtray, and slurp his coffee. Sometimes I would go to Sunday 7:30 mass with Grandma, Uncle Al, and my sister Darlyn. On returning home, we would have donuts and coffee, and since coffee is a grown-up drink, I would have a small amount of coffee with a lot of sugar. When relatives would visit on Sunday night, Grandma would serve boiled hot dogs with homemade apple pie with a slice of sharp cheese on top. I thought it was strange when she placed slices of cheese on the pie, but when on a cracker with jam, it was delicious.

Easter was extra special when all of the grandchildren would receive a huge chocolate Easter rabbit. They would be all lined up on her old cupboard in the back kitchen, and I could not wait to get mine. Christmas would top Easter when we would go to midnight mass and then come back to the old farmhouse and have nuts, cookies, crackers, cheese, liver sausage, and her famous hot chocolate. The next morning would be the opening of presents.

On Saturday nights, I would watch the Lawrence Welk show with her and sometimes during the week General Hospital. Many times, she would be crocheting a beautiful afghan and then give them away at Christmas. My husband uses one to this day when he takes a nap late in the afternoon. It was always fun to be at Grandma Brown's side whether she was preparing a meal or resting on the front porch beside the beautiful geraniums in the flower box. Sometimes I would watch her as she put on makeup and jewelry getting ready for an evening of Bingo. Sometimes I would ride my bike to Grandmas and ride around her driveway just for something different to do and once ending up in the big snowball bush she had at the end of the clothesline. I never told her about damaging her bush! Or I would sneak upstairs in the barn, just playing and hoping to find some great treasure.

The Old Brown Table was a witness to all of these fond memories at what I recall as the Magic Kingdom of Grandma Brown's. Today that Old Brown Table resides in my country kitchen witnessing my family's daily events.

Ref: Marilyn Costa Pocock (Grandchild).

Oh Tara, You Should Be Ashamed of Yourself!

My Aunt Eleanor and Uncle Manny lived next door to Grandma Brown on Route 19, just two miles south of Le Roy. A small field separated the two homes with knee-high grass, some apple trees, and a well-worn meandering path that cut a crooked swath as human tracks tend to do. The trail was a testament to the frequent traffic between the two homes. These were the days when many families just built their new home next door to their parents, as Eleanor and Manny did.

My Aunt had two boys, two girls, and a long lineage of pet dogs for David, their youngest. David loved beagles, and he was very creative with names, like the name "Snoopy." Every new beagle was named Snoopy. Snoopy loved to wander and explore the homestead and beyond, as beagles tend to do. Unfortunately, the Route 19 traffic frequently "collided" with David's roving dogs, resulting in a new Snoopy to replace the void and loss of the recently deceased. We lost count of how many Snoopy's made their home with David and family.

Tara was the break in the Snoopy dynasty and was also the most memorable of David's beagles. Tara was an amiable dog loved by the entire family. She had a beautiful fur coat colored tan with white and black contrast, and irresistible big brown beagle eyes. Now Tara loved table scraps, what beagle doesn't, so Manny and Eleanor gave her a generous daily portion. On quiet summer evenings, her belly satisfied with leftovers from home, she would wander between the walls of green, up the path between the homes, and beg for more at the kitchen door. There she would find solace from my Uncle Al, who just couldn't resist the sad, sorry gaze of seemingly poor, hungry Tara. Those empty yet sparkling beagle eyes easily convinced Alfred that his sister Eleanor was not feeding Tara well enough. So, Al would remedy the situation, filling her plate of dinner food at the foot of the Old Brown Table.

As summer turned to autumn, and the apple trees between the homes grew heavy with fruit, Tara grew heavy as well; so fat that she struggled to navigate the path from her home to Grandma Browns. Her belly would glide along the soft trampled way and eventually find rest in the cool narrow nook beside the outside steps and the cellar doors. A quick whimper announced her readiness to summit the three concrete steps to the kitchen. After another easily teased meal from Uncle Al, she would rest outside as the muggy autumn days welcomed dusk. There, her trophy belly received frequent rubs from the grandchildren who burned off the last of the day's energy, circling the farmhouse with games of hide and seek, before settling in for another quiet evening.

Now a problem arose because Tara became so obese, she could no longer climb the stairs. Seven steps were necessary to enter her house and three steps to enter Grandma's house. To solve the problem, Manny built a handicap ramp for Tara so she could leave and enter their home with a limited strain upon her heart and hips. At Grandma's house, upon hearing that familiar whimper, Uncle Al would lift Tara into the kitchen where another plate of scraps awaited her.

Tara was the first of David's beagles not hit and killed by a car on Route 19. She was simply too obese to wander beyond the path between the two homes and too distracted by dinner scraps, belly rubs, and cool evening naps to make her way anywhere else. There are some advantages of eating to the point of obese. Tara made the most of it by living out a dog's life between cycles of daylight and dinner, with Uncle Alfred by her side at the Old Brown Table.

Ref: Bob Baroncinni (Brown)(Grandchild)

Over the River and Through the Woods

Our four boys were always excited to travel to Grandma Brown's house during those precious years when they were children. The trip would take about five hours over Interstate 90, and of course, the boys would get quite bored exclaiming from time to time, "Are we there yet?". We would take breaks to soothe their anxiousness and run off their energy if that was ever possible. Their dog Corky would be snuggled in the back seat more than happy to travel as long as the boys were present. Trips were quite different than when they were infants when the trunk was filled with diapers, baby food, Similac, and a bottle warmer.

The trips over special holidays such as Easter, Thanksgiving, and Christmas were marked with additional excitement, mainly the exchange of gifts at Christmas. Easter was distinctive as well since Grandma Brown would always give the boys a huge chocolate bunny, those kinds where the feet and head were solid chocolate. We would always color at least five dozen eggs and make one egg a dark muddy black, which was forever given to Uncle Al, just to see him laugh. When going to church, the boys would light candles, and they were amazed at the large display of candles and the beautiful arrangement of Easter lilies.

Christmas at Grandma Browns

One Christmas, we decided to bring Christmas dinner in the 1975 Dodge van, all prepared and ready to place on the Old Brown Table at Grandma's house. We had with us the roasted stuffed turkey, mashed potatoes, yams, string bean casserole, corn, and Italian bread. The forecast was checked the night before and snow was expected along Interstate 90 on the east side of Cleveland, which meant the highway could be very hazardous. We had learned over the years how treacherous this route could be in the dead of winter. So, we planned to travel on regular roads to just south of Erie and join up there with IS 90 toward Buffalo. However, approaching Erie, we found out IS 90 was closed, so we ended up taking regular roads through Pennsylvania and New York arriving at Grandmas around 8 PM, which was six hours late. The late Christmas dinner at the Old Brown Table tasted extra special that year and Grandma, as usual, had made strawberry shortcake with whipped cream.

In the winter at Grandmas, the four boys amused ourselves playing board games, and after tiring would explore the upstairs and the attic seeing what old item could be found among Grandmas rejects. They would love to listen to Grandma's old stories when she was a youth many years ago during times much foreign to them. Uncle Al would sit in the corner smoking his pipe and now and then letting out a hearty laugh from something one of the boys would question. In the evening, after watching TV, Grandma would always prepare a colossal ice cream sundae with chocolate syrup and peanuts on top. Before retiring to the upstairs bedrooms, she would make hot chocolate accompanied alongside cheese and crackers.

In the summer, the boys would explore the red barn, which held many antiques like the wicker wheelchair, and sit-down potty chair. Old tools hung on the barn walls, which had long ago served a purpose on the farm. Then came the long walks in the woods, carving their names on trees and exploring a neighbor's junk pile that held attractive empty crocks of food items many years past.

Those were beautiful days traveling over the river and through the woods to Grandma's house. Days always to be remembered by the boys and, of course, the Old Brown Table. Days now and then recalled as if it had occurred only yesterday.

Ref: Mary Ann Brown

Weapons of Choice

Snowball fights at Grandma Browns were a tradition with the four Brown brothers with the cooperation of the New York winters providing well packed snow. I remember one time when the four of us were having a grandiose snowball fight across the front yard of the old farmhouse. During the heat of battle, I took aim at Dickie and Bobby, both ducking, and the snowball shattering the glass of Grandma's front storm door. I sure got an earful from Dad while in the process of replacing the glass. I could not understand what the big deal was since nobody went through the front door of the house and instead used the side door off the back kitchen. Why couldn't Dad just put a piece of cardboard over the glass opening and called it finished. But what do I know at the age of six?

One time while exploring the farmhouse upstairs, I discovered a strange looking lamp with a large purple bulb. Curious I plugged it in and enjoyed the warm purple glow since it was a cold winter day. However, the next day everyone was curious as to where I got my sunburn. Only I, my brothers and the Old Brown Table knew.

Now my favorite boyhood weapon was the BB gun which I and my three brothers were allowed to shoot at Grandmas. The farmhouse was out in the country without any close neighbors and we could set up targets just about anywhere in the backyard. I became a little adventurous on one occasion and found a spray can in the rickety shed containing various equipment and hardware as well as paints from past projects. I decided to use a spray can as a target against the shed and assumed it was empty. However, I found out the hard way when after taking the shot, hitting the can I could hear a faint sound of hissing and a mist of black paint slowly covering the side of the shed. After quick assessment of the situation I strategically placed some fencing and shrubbery over the spray painted shed and disposed of the spray can in the woods. Thereby the spray paint incident was never mentioned and punishment was circumvented. Not even the Old Brown Table knows!

Now the Brown farmhouse and barn was a haven for a boy yearning for trouble. The red barn was the first place I would run upon arrival from the long trip from Ohio. After the ceremonial hugs and kisses and cheek squeezing by the older girls, I'd run to the red barn sometimes accompanied by the rasp bark of David's glutinous beagle, Tara. Her belly would drag on the ground in a proud display of a dog-years' worth of table scraps. The barn was where my adventures and creativity would be free. It was filled with relics such as Grandpa Brown's Model A doodlebug, antiques, strange looking tools and a large sharpening stone operated by two pedals. I could get that sharpening stone turning very fast with a great deal of momentum. You would be surprised how fast you could turn a piece of scrap metal or wood into a weapon of choice such as a sword, dagger or clever. Hiding those creations involved additional visits to the woods. I'm quite sure, years later, someone on a hike came across my hidden collection and may have thought to search for a corpse nearby.

Now Sunday morning was always special because we would always dress up and attend the church that Dad attended as a small boy. There we would see the same old priest who would never smile. After church we would drive out of the way to pass by Dad's old country school house in the middle of nowhere, a place called Jug City. Everything had a routine during our visits to Grandma Browns. We would always have late night snacks and usually ham for the holiday dinners. Then upon returning home we would always have ham and butter sandwiches Grandma would make accompanied of course with her decadent chocolate cookies. By this time, we already had our fill of her homemade peanut butter, sugar and chocolate cookies from her flowered cookie jar which never became empty. When I see this flowered cookie jar in my home today it forever brings back these cherished memories.

Ole Flowered Cookie Jar

Ref: Christopher Baroncini (Brown) (Grandchild).

"Oh, give thanks to the Lord; call upon his name;
Make known his deeds among the peoples!"
Psalm 105:1

Epilogue

Small towns change with time like everything else, and Le Roy is no exception. Many business establishments have come and gone over the past one hundred years, reusing storefronts several times over. Some buildings have been demolished and replaced with a modern motif, while others have gained a new life through renewal. When one visits the town after several years of absence, nostalgia grips one's memory as to what existed during our Le Roy years.

The Le Roy Theatre, which no longer displays a marquee, has been replaced as the Living Waters Church.

The Dinner Bell restaurant building demolished and replaced with the Tompkins Bank of Castile.

The J.C. Murphy & Co. 5&10 occupied by the Town of Le Roy offices with the store entryway inscribed "J C Murphy Co."

The Blue Bus terminal and the adjoining red brick Masonic Temple replaced with Walgreens Pharmacy.

Memories of days long past now replaced with new experiences of days to come.

"A generation goes, and a generation comes,
    But the earth remains forever,
The sun rises, and the sun goes down,
    And hastens to the place where it rises,
The wind blows to the south
    And goes around to the north;
Around and around goes the wind,
    And on its circuits, the wind returns.
All streams run to the sea,
    But the sea is not full.'
To the place where the streams flow,
    There they flow again."

Ref: Ecclesiastes 1:4-7

SOLO DEO GLORIA

About the Author

William J. Brown is a graduate of the University of Buffalo School of Engineering and served in the USAF for five years at Wright Air Development Division, followed by 31 years at the NASA Glenn (Lewis) Research Center in Cleveland, OH. He authored several technical papers and the Hydrogen & Oxygen Safety manuals retiring in 1993. In 2016 he wrote the book, "My Son, My Son, Where Are You?", in 2017 the book, "A World War I Soldier And His Camera," and in 2018 the book, "The Atom Plane and the Young Lieutenant." He has been married to his wife Mary Ann for 60 years, has four sons, Frank, Richard, Robert, Christopher, 12 grandchildren, and five great-grandchildren.

Connect with the Author

I appreciate you reading my fourth book! Here are social media coordinates:

Visit my website: https://huronbill.wixsite.com/mysite
See me on https://facebook.com/huronbill/

Please read my book published in June 2016 titled, "My Son, My Son, Where Are You?" It is available on Amazon.com in a print and Kindle format and also on Smashwords.com in an eBook format. A true story of an American soldier in WWII told through 500 letters written to the family back home who gave their utmost for the love of God, family, and country. Staff Sergeant Frank W. Brown, a member of the greatest generation, gave his life for the freedoms we enjoy today in a world conflict that affected millions of people. He was a soldier in the 12th Infantry Regiment and trained as a warrior for three years before meeting their foe in the battle of Europe. A genuinely spiritual person who accepted the hardships of life with optimism and heartfelt joy of God's will. When D-Day occurred on June 6, 1944, contact was lost, and two months passed without knowing where Frank was and what happened. His mother continued to write letters every three days until she received official notification on August 6, 1944, that he was killed in action on June 8. A truly inspiring story of courage at home and on the front lines with the sorrow of losing a son.

My second book published in June 2017 titled, "A World War One Soldier and His Camera" is a true story of an American soldier in World War I, who at the rank of Private in 1918, helped to bring the Great War to an end. Emil F. Rezek enlisted in the Navy, became completely bored and wanted out. He took off his sailor's uniform, put on his civies, and enlisted in the Army. After being sent to St. Nazaire, France, as part of the 19th Engineers, he found his mark as an army railroad fireman. However, the Navy MP's caught up with him and was ready to charge him with desertion. Yet, since his commanding officer highly regarded him, he was assigned to the Navy to transport the newly constructed 14 Inch/ 50 Caliber Railroad Gun to the front. In constant danger, five guns were sent to the front lines to shell the German communications and assembly areas. This operation from September to November 1918 was a significant factor in bringing the four-year war to an end with the signing of the armistice on November 11, 1918. The story shows that a soldier in the lowest grade, determined to provide his all, can make a difference. Pvt. Emil Rezek was an avid photographer with his Kodak vest pocket camera, which along with his diary, thoroughly enriches the story. Pvt. Rezek survived the war without any serious injury and returned to the USA, working 45 years as an engineer on the Baltimore & Ohio railroad.

My third book, published in October 2018 titled, "The Atom Plane and the Young Lieutenant," is a true story, which can now be told about the United States Air Force nuclear-powered bomber and the vital role provided by the Wright Air Development Division. The author was privileged to play an engineering role in the testing of critical components of the General Electric X-211 nuclear turbojet during his military service at Wright Patterson Air Force Base in Dayton, OH. Very little is known today about the Aircraft Nuclear Propulsion project, which spanned ten years and the expenditure of one billion dollars. The project was a highly advanced technology program conducted during the 1950's Cold War to provide a continuous 30-day flying bomber ready to respond to any attack on the United States. The mission objectives presented an enormous engineering challenge since an airplane has a critical weight limitation, unlike a nuclear-powered submarine or aircraft carrier, which can accept heavy reactor shielding. High turbojet and reactor material temperature combined with nuclear radiation led to the necessity for significant advancement in technology. Although the nuclear-powered bomber never became an operational weapon system, the technology advancement was a pivotal contribution to our nation's military and civilian air and space programs. Advanced propulsion concepts were also being pursued in the field of nuclear fusion and electro-propulsion for application to air and space missions. The author complements the story with several exciting experiences at Wright Patterson Air Force Base, including aircraft and security incidents, along with a flying saucer investigation. These were indeed, adventurous years exploring the challenge of the unknown.

Notes

Made in the USA
Columbia, SC
27 June 2022